Alex & William,
I hope this will
you ~~both~~ become
"influencers in your field."
You have a wonderful mother (in-law)!
~~Best~~ wishes
Patrick Mayfield.

Practical People Engagement

Leading Change through the Power of Relationships

Patrick Mayfield

Practical People Engagement - Leading Change through the Power of Relationships
Patrick Mayfield

Copy Editor: Elaine Taylor
Cover Design: Mila Perry
Interior Design: Patrick Mayfield

Published in the United Kingdom by Elbereth Publishing
ISBN 978-0-9927114-1-2

Imprint 2

Praise for Practical People Engagement

"This is a veritable feast of practical ideas; it is easy to understand and read. As a reader I felt it had distilled a vast body of knowledge and processed it on my behalf."

— Rick Price
MD of Human Insights

"This is an excellent book – well written, easy to read and pitched at just the right level. It is an excellent source for those that wish to master the art of Stakeholder Engagement."

— Victor Page
DSDM Consortium

"I believe this book could really take the discipline forward and offer an incredibly valuable resource for project managers. A good easy read but with a huge amount of depth. I liken the flow and style to Daniel Pink and Malcolm Gladwell."

— David Elverson
Change Consultancy

"Overall a great read and broad coverage of the subject."

— Stephen Jenner
**Author of *Managing Benefits*
and co-author of *Management of Portfolios***

"As an expert practitioner in the art of learning as well as in project and programme management Patrick has managed, in this book, both to illuminate and to make accessible this much neglected topic. This is the book I always wanted to write - I heartily recommend it to everyone who is striving to deliver significant change."

— Stewart Rapley
Paraclete Consulting

"Something I have enjoyed immensely is that it is as if Patrick is chatting to his readers – huge engagement with the readers!"

— Anne Bellingan
pearcemayfield trainer

"I like the book: It meets a clear and specific need, it is rich in content and experience, it is easy to read and about the right length, and it is well structured – principles, steps, practices/(templates and tools)"

— Keith Williams
Global Consulting Services Executive, APMG International

"I found it really interesting and very helpful.
I suspect that this means that
a) it's well written, and
b) I am rather sad if reading it on South West Trains
means that I put aside my Graeme Greene!"

— Bruce Tanner
UK Foreign and Commonwealth Office

"I enjoyed the book. Lots of good practical
advice which is 'what it says on the tin.'"

— Arnab Banerjee
Programme Manager, Transport for London

"In this age of technology overload, it is refreshing to re-focus on
what makes the greatest difference: human relationships. This
book offers a wealth of guidance and techniques for all change
agents, significantly enhancing established project and programme
management methodologies . A truly valuable resource."

— Nathalie Collister
Chief Examiner, Stakeholder Engagement, APMG International

To Fizz
with eternal appreciation

To Bou, Clara, Scarlett, Elias, Luther and Joy

who each remind me why face-to-face still matters

Contents

[About the Author]

Patrick Mayfield set up and led the first private sector PRINCE–based Project Office at BT Yellow Pages. He was a key member of the team that delivered the first edition of PRINCE2® in 1996. He went on to found pearcemayfield in 2001, of which he has since been a director. He has been writing a blog, *Learning Leader*, since 2004. Also he was a co-author of the *Managing Successful Programmes (MSP)*[1] 2007 edition. He is a member of the Association for Project Management.

Foreword 1.0

T he research undertaken by Patrick Mayfield and John Edmonds into high-performing project and programme managers led to a number of surmises. One of the most important was that such project and programme management (PPM) specialists spent much more time than the average respondent dealing with people and people issues.

This has led to Patrick taking a look at the theory and practice of dealing with people or, as it is more frequently referred in the PPM literature, stakeholder engagement. Patrick has hit on a topic which is very close to the hearts of both experienced and inexperienced PPM specialists. The expression that, "all would be easy in the PPM world if it weren't for the stakeholders" is a long-held belief and Patrick has addressed this with great expertise and more than a little sensitivity. After all, those we seek to persuade, and with whom we seek to engage, are people with feelings, beliefs, attitudes and misconceptions, just like any diverse group of people.

This book provides the reader with a set of seven principles which are in accordance with the best practice principles (as defined by Stephen Covey), namely that they are universal, self-validating and empowering. These form the firm foundation of a set of techniques and practices that provides an armoury of tools which the PPM professional, and others with an interest in dealing with people, can use to attack the stakeholder issues.

It is not an academic book; there are already plenty of those, although it does reference academic literature to support its tenets. Instead it is a really practical guide to assist people to get into the higher ranks of the best-performing PPM specialists. If other professions and activities find use in it too, then I am sure Patrick will not object. This book is of significant value and use to anyone involved in dealing with people in an environment where a common course of action from a diverse set of individuals is the desired result.

Andy Taylor, Aquila Business Services Ltd.

Foreword 2.0

Most of us know that stakeholder engagement is a vital part of delivering change, but then most of us think that it is just difficult. So, we retreat into a position of 'doing the least possible', meeting the requirements of the method or model that we are using in a way that 'ticks the box'.

This book is a delightful antidote to that approach.

It is full of really useful ideas and practices, expressed in a way that is extremely understandable. The overall structure of the book helps enormously, yet the structure does not become the dominant factor.

Practical People Engagement is an important and very practical contribution to the world of project, programme and change management – keep it on your desk at all times!

John Edmonds, Head of Training, pearcemayfield & Founder of *Roots*

Preface

I came into the change business through project management, the hard way, without books, without training, learning on the job, from my own mistakes. I realise now that life was kind to me. Like a smoker in a dynamite factory, I got away with it, mostly. There were no disasters but there were delays and disappointments.

In the late 1980's I was head of IT Development in a regional government when I heard of PRINCE, a project management methodology owned by the UK Government. This set me on a track that led to my being invited onto the project that delivered the first version of PRINCE2®[2] in 1996. The people aspects were still marginal in that first edition. However, at that time all the standard project management references treated the human issues that way, if at all.

Ten years later, my colleagues and I began to track an exciting pattern. Staying close to our customers we found that how project managers approached the 'people thing' was a *key indicator of their performance*. We found similar results reported by Andy Crowe[3]. Without a doubt, the better regarded project managers tended to approach relationships in and around their projects in a quite different way.

This book began to grow out of the material for a workshop we developed called Engaging Your Project Stakeholders. As I compiled notes on this much-neglected topic, I was struck by the power and richness of the material. As we delivered the workshop the response was even more powerful. People were impressed with the results of connecting with others who mattered in a project in different ways. We realised that what we had called the 'Communications Plan' within PRINCE2 had become something quite arid, even yet another barrier to true engagement.

---

2   PRINCE2® is a Registered Trademark of AXELOS Limited.
3   *Alpha Project Managers: What the Top 2 Per Cent Know That Everyone Else Does Not* (Velociteach Press, 2006).

Later, John Edmonds and I ran a research project around the behaviours of high-performing programme and project managers. There was a discussion going around the Internet at the time that argued, "If only we could get into the minds of high performers, and see what mental checklists or crib sheets these champions used, we could reproduce their results by following the same lists." Our research questions were, "Did all high-performers have such lists?", and "If so, are they the same?" We called it the Crib Sheet project .

What surprised us was the strength of one of the findings that emerged: as measured in the proportion of their discretionary time, the higher performers all exhibited a strong leaning to relationships. They spent more time with people: 40-60% of their discretionary time on average compared to 10-12% for the rest of the population. From subsequent interviews this appeared to be quite a conscious and intentional choice. And it delivered results, it seemed. We were onto something.

Now I see the need for this kind of approach almost daily in my work. It seems to have been "hiding in plain sight." Therefore I felt this material deserved a wider audience.

Who I was thinking of when I wrote this

At a recent conference where I spoke on stakeholder engagement, there was general agreement that project managers among others needed a decent treatment of this subject from their perspective. So I wanted to create a practical guide to the subject of engaging with people, often called 'stakeholder management'. I've written this primarily for project managers, leading change through a project. However, some reviewers of early drafts of this book urged me to position it as relevant for all involved in driving change, even those executing strategy at senior levels.

In essence, if you are responsible in any way for seeing new outcomes emerge in any organisation - for bringing in new practices or ways of seeing or doing things - you will find this of value. In fact, there is an emerging role among operational managers of being change leaders. If you are someone who finds yourself on the receiving end of project delivery, and finding yourself persuading the people you work with to use and exploit that new thing the project has delivered – or is about to - this book will help you a great deal.

My aim has been to give you a clear, practical reference which helps you improve the performance of leading any kind of change, project-based or otherwise.

As a convention, I use the term 'project'. In most cases this is equally applicable - sometimes even more so - to larger transformational change, sometimes called 'programmes' (or 'programs'), that coordinate several projects, and to the whole high-level enterprise that is now called portfolio management.

This Books is not meant to be...

- **Academic.** I've written it to offer practical help. Research is referenced, but I take a stance from practical experience. If this means that any particular area or approach is ignored, then please write and tell me[4].

- **Culturally universal.** With the rise of global projects, international cultural differences need to be taken into account. There are others better qualified to write on engaging with people from diverse international cultures. I do not mean to diminish the importance of differences in regional cultures, but this book is focused on what I perceive as generic, universal issues, ones common to all cultures, to all humans.

- **Exhaustive.** One consultant I know, whenever we disagree, often responds like this: "Well, we are all the sum of our own experiences". He does have a point. I'm very conscious that I've omitted techniques and practices valued by many. Some of my reviewers told me as much. Also, I'm sure that there are techniques out there that I should have included that will only come to my attention after this is published. (My unconscious incompetence.) So be it. This book can't include everything. People engagement is a large and rich field. So I have attempted the Pareto Principle: include that 20% that will help you 80% of the way.

Harwell, Oxfordshire, UK

August 2013

---

4 You can reach me via Twitter @PatrickMayfield

Foundations

In this opening section we explore what's lacking in current approaches, consider a broader landscape of people engagement, and set out the seven principles of engagement.

CHAPTER 1

A better way

Out of clutter, find simplicity.
From discord, find harmony.
In the middle of difficulty lies opportunity.

—Albert Einstein

The onslaught of change

In terms of the numbers of people involved, project management is going from strength to strength. More people now, than ever before, are being asked to manage projects. This is hardly surprising. Our generation has witnessed an explosion of change. And projects are still the main vehicles for delivering that change.

As a consequence, change management is also in the ascendant. Change managers, perhaps more than their project management colleagues, recognise and address the communications and engagement challenges around any initiative that drives a major change.

Yet when it comes to actual practice there seems to be a widespread culture of learned helplessness, where managers show a growing lack of confidence in their plans being met, and where failing to meet the business case is seen as usual.

Something is missing

A man finds a drunk one night crawling around a lamppost. "What are you doing?" he asks.

"Looking for my keys."

"Did you drop them here?"

"No," he replied, "over there, but the light is better over here."

I have a growing conviction that we have been looking for answers in the wrong places. All too often the treatment of relationships with people within and around a project is sporadic and marginal, a sort of afterthought from the 'core' issues of network diagrams, Gantt charts, work breakdown structures, user requirement specifications , and so on. The light seems to be better over there.

Many managers I meet still seem to see the business of leading people as at best, marginal to the challenge of driving change through. Engaging and influencing people has been seen as a sort of sideshow to the 'real' practice of managing projects. At worst, it has been dismissed as being too 'soft', an embarrassing subject to proper business people, definitely not something to get in the way of 'hard' technical execution.

How to waste £billions

But what really happens if you ignore relationships on a project? What would happen if you did not do any significant engagement with people outside of formal progress meetings?

You don't need to look too far for the answer. I have seen project managers at every level who focus exclusively on the traditional technical elements. There seems to be a conspiracy from all quarters – much of academia, journals, auditors, much of the discussion within professional bodies, and tools vendors – that process, task, and documents are of supreme importance, it seems.

As a consequence many people who should be involved instead feel neglected. This encourages fear, and sometimes anger. Non-cooperation and resistance grows. The project may complete and the manager moves on, feeling that they have delivered to contract. But what of the expected positive outcomes set out in the business case? These are usually absent and there is often a bow wave of resentment and poor performance in the wake of the project.

Unless your project is building something simple to a customer's clear, stable brief, inattention to the people issues will result in a host of problems and disappointment.

> One client told me that his organisation decided to replace an internal stock fulfilment system that had become redundant to needs. So he went to one independently minded operations manager to explain the plan, how he would be impacted, how he would benefit and so on.
>
> Not long into the conversation, he interrupted with: "Oh well, we never did use the old system anyway!"
>
> I'm not sure which is more shocking: that this had only just come to light, or that the previous project never did engage with this manager. The result was that, although the previous system had been delivered, it had never been exploited in this area of the organisation, benefits had not been realised and the business case had not been met. And no one seemed to know this.

Is this an extreme example? Perhaps. However, in our practice we have found many other examples of poor engagement leading to delay, frustration, additional cost, and poor, or non-existent benefit realisation. If we could measure the consequential waste it would be staggering.

Here's another example offered by one of my reviewers, David King:

> "In the early 1990's I went to interview the Director of a UK Government department's business unit to do a PIR (post-implementation review) of an office automation (OA) project, an early implementation of a fully networked office IT solution, only to discover the Director sat at his desk using one of the spanking new stand-alone PCs that had started to become available.

> "The OA terminal sat behind him, dusty and unused. This was hardly role modelling the expected use of the implemented system, which had, unsurprisingly, fallen into disuse, after only 6 months. "

One study in the UK[1], suggested that the problem is less to do with 'core' project management and more to do with a lack of commitment around the project *after* it delivers, amounting to £50bn per annum in the UK in lost benefits in the IT sector alone. This huge waste is largely attributable to poor relationship management with key people.

The better way

The opposite also happens: engage people early, ably and continuously - well before delivery, even before a project is launched - and the best outcome is more likely. More than that, we have seen projects and their related operational changes exceed planned benefit realisation, particularly where key people around the project have worked creatively to identify and realise additional, unforeseen benefits.

These positive cases are where leaders engage people well, involving them appropriately and in a timely manner. Every one of these leaders has a clear idea of what they need from each person, during and beyond the project. They have a plan for taking people through the journey of the change. Those affected are treated with consideration and dignity, led to better places, supported along the way.

---

1   Quoted by Gerald Bradley in *Benefits Realisation Management: A Practical Guide to Achieving Benefits through Change*, page 1.

As mentioned earlier, we have found that managers who are regarded as the most capable, spend significantly more time in purposeful conversations with people than the rest.

> "There are two kinds of project manager: the ones who do what the book says. You will find them at their desk working on their plans and reports. But the really useful kind is never at their desks; they are out meeting with people, making things happen."

Website manager for a global media business.

The reason the higher performers show this relational leaning is because it gets results. It works. By focusing on relationships with key people these higher performers find that it actually pays dividends, saving time and cost later, as well as driving up customer perceived value.

The Value Ladder

There is a vital value ladder that looks like this:

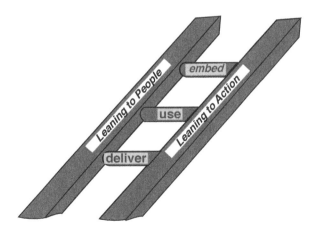

Figure 1 : Value Ladder

The value ladder focuses on three major milestones:

- When the new thing is **delivered**.

- When it is commissioned and actively **used**.

- When it is so **embedded** in practical use that it becomes the new 'normal', and benefits are consequentially, consistently and optimally realised.

The ladder has two supports throughout this climb: a **leaning to relationships** and a **leaning to action**. Unless the steps are supported by both of these, an organisation cannot rise to beneficial outcomes; change never gets beyond delivery. Whilst this does not all rest on the project manager's shoulders, those of us leading projects can do much to ensure the climb to value is possible.

Turning into the skid

I bought my first car when I was a student in Scotland. It was a rear-wheel drive Hillman Minx. It was a rust-bucket, but I loved it. I also remember my first skid in the snow. My father, who grew up driving tractors on my grandfather's farm, always told me: "Steer into a skid." It felt counter-intuitive, but it worked of course. I felt the car come back on track.

For many people, when they are up against the clock the last thing they want to consider is spending time on the "people thing". It seems to be counter-intuitive to many managers. This is understandable. Most project management texts seem to major on the project as a set of tasks and process. People seem to get in the way of the smooth running of the project. Spending valuable time on communicating with people in and around the project feels counter-intuitive, like turning into a skid.

On the contrary, what many have found is that if 'relationship time' is done in a consistent, thoughtful and intentional manner, it can actually save time, reduce risk and waste, and can even give the business case a boost. The time invested in relationships begins to correct the project when it goes into a skid. Frequently I have found people have rallied to me and helped when new issues arose. It seems that they are returning the relational investment I have put into them.[2]

I'm not that type of person

At this point you may be thinking, "Well, that may be true, but that's not the kind of person I am. I'm not a people person."

Neither am I. Personality profiles have, at various times, labeled me "Introvert" and "Matter Attached". Yet I have learned to work with the larger reality: the reality that relationships are more important than most realise. The sub-title for this book could have been "what one introvert learned the hard way".

In the following pages, allow me to introduce you to some key ideas that will help you, such as:

- Scaling engagement through your team

- How the "extroverts" among us are not necessarily the most influential personality types

- How we all can summon courage to "walk across the room" to engage with people

- Simple conversational techniques that can alter someone's attitude.

Join me on this journey, exploring the many ways we can appropriately engage with people. You will begin to see it as feasible for yourself, whatever your situation. By taking small steps towards engagement you are likely to find that it has a positive impact on you personally.

---

2   Robert Cialdini explores the principle of reciprocity in his *Influence: The Psychology of Persuasion* as the reciprocal effect. (Harper Collins: 2007).

Some definitions

We can't get very far without defining our terms.

Stakeholder

What do we mean by the word 'stakeholder'?

A common definition of a 'stakeholder' is any individual or group that has an interest in or some influence over the project or its outcome. That's a pretty broad definition, isn't it?

And since we are dealing with definitions …

'Stakeholder Engagement'

There is a fundamental problem with the more common term 'Stakeholder Management.'

First, if you go with the above definition of stakeholders (anyone interested in the project or its outcome) then it is bound to include people over whom you have no direct authority: people from other departments, even outside of your organisation. Changes of any size have always cut across business functions, organisation boundaries, across silos of working, so the more successful ones deal with this reality by engaging with people. In a strict sense, these are not people you can 'manage', nor should you try.

Second, I have concerns with the very concept of 'managing' people, particularly managing knowledge workers, however deeply entrenched that language may be in business. We manage things, we manage a production line, we manage non-human resources. But we lead people, we direct people, we motivate people, we enlighten people, we coach people, we learn with people. We don't manage them. Taking the very term 'stakeholder management' on board all too easily seduces us into thinking that it is legitimate and feasible to process human beings, to manipulate them to get the right response.

This idea of management comes largely from an extension of the profound historical influence of Frederick Taylor and his principles of production management. Taylor's principles were highly successful in manufacturing, but are largely delusional when it comes to the matter of dealing with human beings with other agendas, loyalties, histories, personalities and power.

In his book *Drive*, Daniel Pink[3] shows that for tasks that are more than merely mechanical, tasks which require some thought, analysis, discretion and creativity, people respond quite differently to incentives. The motivations are often more intrinsic, about the meaning of the work, the autonomy given to the worker, and the sense of mastery gained. This reveals a truth that is unwelcome to many a busy manager: people are complex, and their behaviours will defy them being reduced to mere resources and to being shuffled about. They need to be engaged.

For these reasons, I prefer the term 'Stakeholder Engagement'. It puts you - uncomfortably perhaps - on a more equal footing with your stakeholders, demanding, for example, that you have conversations with them, conversations that may well have unknown results, conversations that will take valuable time. However, if you take on this new perspective[4], most people will respond very positively. The potential is enormous. It can unlock 'people power' towards achieving your goal.

You will probably save time, remove impediments to progress, and find that the momentum gathers, the pace accelerates.

Start where you are

Perhaps you have picked this book up because you are in the middle of a change initiative or project, and people are getting upset or causing you problems. In which case, I advise you to dip in wherever your current problem is, and come back to the other parts of this book later. For example, in the pathway section, at the end of each chapter, there are indicators that suggest when you should use that particular step.

Flexibility is so important. With people engagement, agility should not be hamstrung by process. Again, don't feel constrained to follow the sequence of the engagement pathway religiously.

Finally, think of many of the practices and techniques in this book more as your learning scaffolding. When you have developed your own structure of competence in stakeholder engagement with your own practices and techniques, you can take down my scaffolding.

---

3   Daniel Pink, *Drive: The Surprising Truth about What Motivates Us*, (Riverhead Books, 2009).

4   This new perspective is explored further in Chapter 2.

A Better Way - Summary

- Successful change is far more than focusing on "stuff": process, documents and techniques

- Failure often occurs after delivery

- People are complex. Deal with this reality

- High performers spend more discretionary time engaging with people, and get results

- Stay flexible in your approach. Treat this material as your temporary scaffolding until you develop your own.

CHAPTER 2

Seeing the bigger picture

As a man thinks, so he is.

—Socrates

And 600 years before Socrates …
As he thinks in his heart, so is he.

—Solomon

What do you notice?

What you believe as being important in leading people through change, what you pay attention to and monitor, is crucial. If you limit yourself to focusing on mechanistic management processes, documents and techniques, you will, at best, only achieve positive results by accident. At worst, your efforts could backfire and cause people to resist even more what you are trying to do.

So I urge you to consider what you actually take notice of, and to consider what you think is important. Also think about the language you use to speak about your work.

Frames of Reference

When you look at this picture, what do you see?

Some see one thing, others another. Some see a young woman looking away over her right shoulder; others see an old woman with a large nose looking down. If you have seen this picture before, someone no doubt has explained it to you, so that you can flip between seeing one image and the other. [Look at the almost-horizontal line towards the bottom of the picture: it's the collar-band of the young woman and the mouth of the old woman.]

[Got it?... OK.]

This is a clever, ambiguous picture, but what is its relevance here? Gestalt psychology demonstrates with images such as this that the human brain makes sense of reality more by interpreting whole patterns rather than individual elements. This has a consequence: we tend to focus on certain matters in the foreground of our consciousness whilst filtering out a lot of other detail, elements that don't fit our structure, leave these unnoticed in the background. In this way, we are told, we all approach reality with our own frames of reference.

Through our training, through life experience, through the use of computer tools, we all have developed a frame of reference that notices certain things in our work; we believe these things matter to the success of the change. In this way, we train our brains to focus on certain data.

Our research confirmed, for example, that not all managers have the same frame of reference. Some see certain things that others miss.

Now this is not merely a matter of personality or taste. Our frames of reference matter to how well we perform in leading change. It seems that some of us have been unaware of some quite important clues. We miss vital evidence.

When you look at your work priorities today, what do you see? What sort of things do you think matter? What are the priorities on your to-do list? What sort of things are mere distractions?

We identified a quite different prevailing frame of reference for the few high performing managers. This difference is largely in the area of people and relationships, of stakeholders and communication. For all too many managers, such things as relationships and conversation are distractions; these just slow them down. So they leave them in the background and focus on other things. And yet the evidence is there: higher performers have a relational leaning, making time for people and relationships.

In the pursuit of becoming a better influencer, a better leader, your self-reflection on this is really quite crucial.

The traditional project management landscape

Project management as a branch of general management has grown out of construction and civil engineering. In the last sixty years there has been a heavy emphasis on project management in the growth of information technology and its application in organisations of all kinds. This has led to a very task and process-oriented view of what matters in projects. This is the orthodox frame of reference. If people have been considered at all within this world view, they have been thought of as 'resources', units to help production.

This way of thinking runs deep. Even if we rationally agree that people matter, we may still find ourselves hunting for the 'right' process model to use, the tasks we should do, and the documents we should create, even the 'app' that we can run to support us. This all misses the essential point in effective stakeholder engagement.

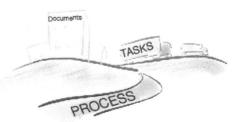

A more inclusive view

The inner circle of the diagram below shows some of the elements that have been traditionally important to managers. The outer circle adds essential elements within a more progressive view of engagement.

By enlarging your focus to include the outer circle, you treat people, not as

Figure 2 : A more inclusive view

fungible resources – things that can be replaced with like for like - nor as objects to be processed, to be broadcast at, but rather as unique human beings, irrational at times, emotional, forgetful, with their own agendas, power, and fears. These are people with whom you can, and sometimes should, have conversations, who may pleasantly surprise you with their responses and ideas.

Some of the terms included in the outer circle might make you feel uneasy. It might seem rather unfamiliar territory. However, the pay-off in performance is considerable. With this larger view, you will find yourself aware of some critically important aspects of change where people are involved. You will notice more. You now 'see' the old woman *and* the young woman. And because you notice more, you engage more effectively.

Again and again leaders with this larger view of things get better results. Whilst it may feel counter-intuitive to try this, you will find that spending more time in purposeful conversations with people will help save time and money. And you are far more likely to delight your customers.

Principles, themes, steps, practices and techniques

In the next chapter we consider seven principles, which provide a clear compass for anyone anywhere in a change. If we follow these principles throughout our engagement journey on a daily basis, we are well on our way to success.

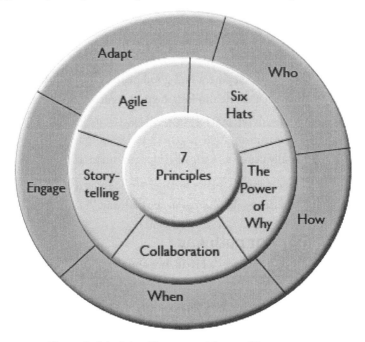

Figure 3 : Principles, Themes and Steps of Engagement

The section that follows is devoted to the major emergent themes in people engagement:

- **The Six Engagement Hats**. The six hats look at the business of engagement from six different viewpoints. Techniques for using these six prevent you from falling prey to tunnel vision. You are more likely to see the whole thing in the round and, as a result, your engagement approach will be more robust.

- **The Power of Why**, the leader's favourite question. The question "Why" relates to a number of facets relevant to understanding the motivations of the people you are seeking to engage.

- **Collaboration** in engagement and some collaboration tools: Collaborative engagement is both a necessity and a key enabler to high performance. What you can do in engagement on your own is limited. Collaborative techniques address that but also mobilise some of the people you are seeking to influence. It gets their 'buy-in' often through sharing a sense of ownership of your change.

- **Story-telling** is such a potent vehicle of engagement that in recent years it has become recognised as a legitimate business tool.

- **Agile**. Agile development and good people engagement go hand in hand. Much of the thinking behind Agile development would not work without good people engagement, but also, we have much to learn from Agile practices and techniques, even if we are not formally using an Agile development method.

These topics emerge as major themes throughout effective engagement and each of them relate to all the steps in the pathway.

The engagement pathway

The final section explores a broad, but simple engagement pathway. This is reduced to five basic steps.

- **Who**. This Step is where you identify and begin to understand the players within and around your change or project, and makes sure you don't make the cardinal error of missing or ignoring someone important. It studies these people and examines their agendas and interests. This intelligence is crucial in adopting the right approach in the next step.

- **How**. This Step helps you shape your overall approach, your strategy of engagement. Given the mix of reactions you can anticipate from different groups, you will find it helpful to decide the sequence of key messages to gain the maximum engagement, impact, co-operation and traction. Here we explore some well-established models of how this sequencing can be done.

- **When**. This Step builds on this broad strategy with a plan of key events and messages, taking people through a purposeful story of change, considering carefully how to 'get through' to particular stakeholders who are likely to be bombarded with all sorts of calls on their attention and time.

- **Engage**. Execution is often missed in theory books in business. Yet it is the most important step of all. Everything else amounts to nothing without looking in the whites of people's eyes and talking with them. This Step is about taking all this theory and preparation, and putting it into practice.

- **Adapt**. This Step is taking account of reality, reviewing what is going on, and taking conscious steps to adjust. Engagement is not an exact science, and feels more like an exploration into the unknown at times. We need to be alert, agile and quick to adapt.

As you use these steps, and their associated practices and techniques, you will become more effective in influencing people and gaining their cooperation in achieving good outcomes.

These steps are in a deliberate sequence. However, I do not recommend you follow this pathway mechanistically. You are not meant to execute one of the steps along the pathway and then forget it, moving on to the next, like a cog turning in a ratchet. This would be too rigid. Rather think of the steps in the pathway more like stepping stones across a fast-flowing stream. You can choose to leap to an alternative stone if the particular conditions at the time suggest it.

If you use this pathway properly, you will find you leap back frequently and go over the same steps again, but this time with more information and experience. If anything, it is better used iteratively than as a linear process.

Nor are these steps of equal importance. The first in the section, the Who Step, is not necessarily the first in importance, but simply where I suggest you might start. (In fact, I think Engage is the most important Step, followed by Adapt and then How.) The pathway does represent a logical sequence where work is built up from the previous steps. However, reality is not that neat and tidy. It is much more volatile and chaotic. The stream that the steps cross floods at times. Often we just need to deal with different challenges as they present themselves.

The practices and techniques

Throughout, but particularly within the pathway, you will find a number of *practices*. These are particular professional approaches that have come from what we have observed among high performers. As you employ these practices, you will find that you engage with people significantly better. More than that, your experience will be so much more positive: you will find that you are more likely to enjoy working with the people around you.

Also, you will find supplemental *techniques*. These are more at the "how to" level, and illustrate the themes, steps and practices in some way.

Not all practices have supporting techniques, and many techniques stand on their own. Whether practices or techniques, it is your choice whether you use them or not. People engagement is as much an art as a science.

Practice: Be clear on the outcome you want [Leader]

For example, here is the first practice, that is familiar to the Leader's perspective[1].

The more progressive mindset includes one particular element: thinking in terms of outcomes. An outcome is the result of what you deliver as an output or set of outputs. One definition of an outcome is "the result of a change, normally affecting behaviours and circumstances of people operating a transformed business", transformed, in our case by the use of something new that is brought into being. Projects, for example, enable outcomes; projects rarely fully deliver outcomes directly.

---

1   See the Leader's Hat in the Six Engagement Hats Chapter.

For example, a project might deliver a new website, the desired outcome might be many visitors to that site, with the benefits being improved page rankings or perhaps increased sales if people can buy through it. We see a simple causal link between these three terms like this:

Figure 4 : The relationship of outputs, outcomes and benefits/goals

This is another way of describing the steps in the value ladder[2], where the

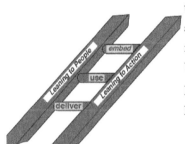

three steps of 'deliver', 'use' and 'embed' are supported throughout by leaning into relationships and leaning to action. Understanding these concepts, though, is perhaps easier than actually changing our professional habits.

Development teams are rightly concerned with the features and specifications of what they have to deliver. However, it seems to come as a surprise to some project managers when they realise that most of the people who will use what is delivered are not particularly interested in its features: they are more likely to be thinking how it will make their lives better or worse, how it will help or hinder their work.

Exercise: So write down what you are going to deliver (your 'output', 'product', or 'deliverable') and then ask, "Why might someone need it?" Then ask yourself, 'So what?' Keep on asking these questions until you have written down benefits or disadvantages to your stakeholders.

Now you are beginning to think more about outcomes and their benefits than merely features and "functionality."

See Chapter 1.

We can begin to use the output-outcome-goal framework to structure our conversations with stakeholders. It is a powerful format of shaping key messages, as we will see later.

Seeing the bigger picture - Summary

So let's summarise the key points of seeing the bigger picture.

- Adopting the right perspective is crucial. Traditional thinking will, at best, only get indifferent results with people

- Be conscious of your frame of reference. Think about your change as more than just tasks, processes, techniques, documents, and general 'stuff'

- Gain clarity about the results your clients want beyond the project. This is essential material for our conversations with people

- Use the output-outcome-benefits/goal model to structure your own thinking and the conversations you have with people you seek to influence

- The engagement principles are together an important compass. Use them to orient yourself on what is important

- The emergent themes are relevant through most of the engagement pathway

- The engagement pathway is not a strict sequence, dip in where your need is at the time

- All steps are not equal. Action, the Engage Step, trumps everything

- Do come back to other parts later

- Do the Adapt Step and you will improve your engagement over time

- Expect to do two or more steps at any given moment.

Seeing the bigger picture - Practice

- Being clear on the outcome you want.

CHAPTER 3

Seven principles of stakeholder engagement

I find the great thing in this world is, not so much where
we stand, as in what direction we are moving.

—Goethe

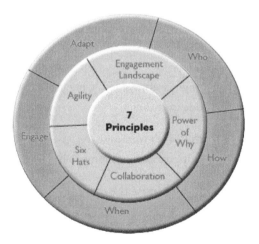

T his chapter introduces the concept of guiding principles and the seven
in stakeholder engagement. These seven principles are referenced
throughout the rest of this book. Use these seven principles as a sort of
running practice checklist.

What is a "principle"?

In his book, *Principle-Centered Leadership*, the late Stephen Covey set out to explain leadership around a set of principles. He defined a principle as:

- **Universal**. A principle will apply anywhere, at any time. It is not something that goes out of fashion, nor is it limited to a particular organisational or geographic culture

- **Self-validating**. As a principle is used it is found to work. Note: Covey did not describe principles as 'self-evident'; fools and novices do not recognise a principle as a principle. So the notion of a principle is that it is empirically proven

- **Empowering**. A principle, when used, gives you leverage over a challenge or problem.

We have identified seven such principles around stakeholder engagement:

1. **Seek first to understand & then be understood.** Listening is always the start position in effective influencing.

2. **Effective change is always led.** Change is so uncertain we need leaders to guide us through.

3. **Habits are the inhibitors and the goal.** Habits make us resist change, and our goal is not to remove habits but to replace them.

4. **Recognise and minimise the pain of change.** People always seek to minimise pain, so engage them with this in mind.

5. **High performance comes through people and action.** Leaning into relationships is a key proclivity for being effective, as is being action-oriented, rather than being continually stuck in analysis.

6. **Integrity is powerfully persuasive.** It breeds trust and makes engagement so much easier.

7. **Feelings trump reason, and meaning trumps authority**. We are not as rational as we like to think we are, and so engagement works better when we recognise the need for emotional connection. Also connecting people to the reasons for change is more helpful than merely wielding authority and commanding people to change.

When we wrote the 2007 edition of *Managing Successful Programmes* (MSP®)[1] we used Covey's definition, and distilled seven principles from case studies and our own experience. The principles are very powerful. We went so far as to say that one could employ these principles and be successful whilst using very different processes, practices and techniques. Processes and techniques are thus secondary; they become the servants of living the principles.

I am acutely aware that many do not teach or practise MSP this way, which is a great pity. It leads to a very deterministic and legalistic interpretation of a truly powerful and flexible framework. The principles should be seen as the centre around which everything else is pivoted. Covey saw a principle as like a compass, always pointing true north: whatever your context, the principle will always orient you.

So let's explore each of these seven principles a little more deeply.

1   *Managing Successful Programmes* (Cabinet Office: TSO, 2011). MSP® is a Registered Trademark of AXELOS Limited. The authoring team was led by Rod Sowden and included Geof Leigh, Chris Venning and me.

1. Seek first to understand ⋯ then be understood

One of the most powerful influencing strategies is to ask the other person for their interests, their needs and their fears first; to be interested genuinely in them and their struggles. The simple courtesy of being interested first in them, of being fully present with them in conversations about them, breaks down more hostility and barriers than anything else I can think of. Listening to others first almost earns us the right to be heard ourselves.

However, this is more than a matter of mere politeness. This principle recognises that no single person or even a small group has a full view of what is actually happening in the organisational system[2]. Understanding how others see a problem is essential if we are to make the right calls.

Also, it fits well with a paradox well known among change leaders:

Never start the conversation with your solution

Rather focus on the need for change. In fact, beginning this way could open the conversation for the other party to propose a better way to meet the change than you had first considered.

So why isn't this being done more often? There could be a number of reasons:

- There is the general issue of **busyness**. People forget in the heat of the moment, seeking to grab the opportunity to make their pitch, get agreement and move on. Trainers can be prone to this, and the training experience suffers because of it. Often we lack the patience to invite opinions, but also we may have an unwillingness to open ourselves to the risk that they may lecture us. We will return to the issues of busyness later in this book.

- There is also the matter of **pride**. Can we humble ourselves and sit with these people and listen to their complaints? I believe this prevents many from getting better at people engagement. We lack the attitude of the servant leader; someone who can lead by serving. If we are willing to stoop to serve, we will make better leaders, and so others will be more inclined to follow us.

---

2   For example, see Oshry's analysis in the How Step.

- Then there is the desire to exert **power and control**. This usually comes from an underlying belief that we know best and that all we need to do is drive the solution through. The approach in this book takes a fundamentally different way of seeing beneficial change happen – working with people through a process of change that seeks to bring people on board. This is much more collaborative.

The Engage Step offers several approaches for engaging with people in this way. One of the most powerful techniques is Active Listening[3]. This goes some way to practising what Daniel Goleman[4] describes as 'social awareness', as one of the key competences of an emotionally intelligent leader.

The other half of this principle is that of knowing the right moment to make our position and needs clear. Going in with what we want first is not a particularly persuasive approach, but knowing when to use a pause and then state our position is also included here.

We have not seen many leaders progress far without living this principle to some extent. Hence it is the first principle.

The power of empathy and the other-perspective

The other-perspective is the ability to 'read' a person, to track their thinking, to discern their underlying motives. Other-perspective is more empathy than sympathy. With sympathy, you take on the feelings of another, even to the extent of adopting their feelings and owning their point of view for yourself. That is not always appropriate or helpful. Empathy, however, is the ability to put oneself in another's shoes.

This is part of what Goleman[5] means by social awareness,. He brings some compelling data to the argument that all great leaders, people who operate at a high level of influence and persuasion, have high emotional intelligence in this respect.

Daniel Pink[6] describes this as a combination of perspective-taking and empathy. In order to influence a person to 'buy' your idea or proposal you need to reduce your power and move to humility. He suggests attention to feelings as well as to rational thinking.

---

3   See Engage! step.
4   *Working with Emotional Intelligence* (Bloomsbury, 1999).
5   Ibid.
6   Daniel Pink, *To Sell is Human: the surprising truth about persuading, convincing and influencing others* (Canongate: 2013).

2. Effective change is always led

If your actions inspire others to dream more, learn more,
do more and become more, you are a leader.

—John Quincy Adams

The first task of a leader is to define reality. The last task
is to say 'thank you', and in between he's a servant.

—Max De Pree

A project is essentially a change vehicle. It brings about change, directly or indirectly, to the people who will be using what you deliver.

What is not so obvious is that we always need leaders in times of change. If all were stable, if there were no change, all we would need would be managers and workers. Change, however, disturbs people's lives; almost always it requires people to alter their behaviours. In taking people out of routine, the future becomes less certain. We need a leader to clarify why and what that future might look like. In these contexts people want to be led. We need leaders more often than we might think.

Leaders set direction, they chart a new course. To engage people effectively you will need to lead. People will expect purpose, meaning, and some sort of picture of the future that you are aiming to realise. Being a role model communicates much of this. Such is the craft of leaders.

"Leader" and "leadership" have some divergent common meanings, and are often confused with management. For our purposes we will use a table from Warren Bennis[7] in order to make this distinction.

---

7   Warren Bennis, *Authentic Leadership: Rediscovering the Secrets to Creating Lasting Value* (Jossey-Bass, 1994).

Bennis proposes, for example, that leaders are more focused on people, whereas a manager focuses primarily on system and structure. If this is the case then, if we want to be at all effective in stakeholder engagement, we need to take on some of the perspectives and behaviours of a leader.

a manager ...	... whereas a leader
administers	innovates
is a copy	is an original
maintains	develops
focuses on system & structure	focuses on people
relies on control	inspires trust
has a short-term view	has a long-range perspective
asks how & when	asks why
has an eye on the bottom line	has an eye on the horizon
imitates	originates
accepts the status quo	challenges the status quo
classic good soldier	own person
does things right	does the right thing
aims for efficiency	aims for effectiveness

Source: Warren Bennis (1994)

Figure 5 : Managers v Leaders

The table does not mean we are either a leader or a manager. All leaders are managers as well, but not all managers are leaders. For example, in the engagement pathway, you will need to ask How and When, so involving a degree of management thinking alongside the leader's perspective.

We will develop the concept of a leader further as one of the key perspectives we need to use in people engagement. It is helpful here, however, to make another point: when we refer to leadership, we are not talking about positional power and authority. Leaders can and should arise in times of change at all levels in an organisation, whatever their power and seniority.

So ask yourself this question: "Are you more used to operating as a manager or a leader?"

3. Habits are the inhibitors and the goal

Good habits are as addictive as bad habits, and a lot more rewarding.

—Harvey Mackay

The chains of habit are too weak to be felt until
they are too strong to be broken.

— Samuel Johnson

When we learn a new skill, it is exhausting. It requires a lot of conscious mental effort, a lot of oxygen to the brain. Hence many people find they are very tired at the end of long meetings, when they apparently have done very little physical activity. This is because they have been working hard with their conscious understanding and behaviours. The conscious area of their brains has been stretched, burning that oxygen.

Enter habits.

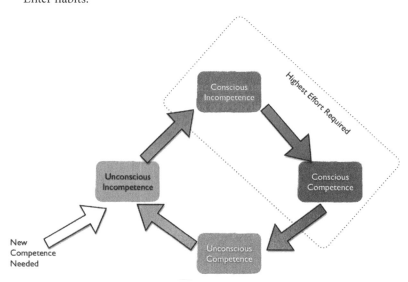

Figure 6 : Competence Cycle and Effort

Habits are what learning psychologists often refer to as unconscious competence or unconscious incompetence. The human brain functions by using a particularly efficient mechanism. It puts learned skills into the background, allowing the scarcer brain real estate of consciousness to attend to other things.

So in one sense the goal of change is to develop new, better habits; to develop new behaviours in people to the point that they no longer notice them.

However, such are the strengths of our old habits and such is the effort we need to summon to develop new ones, we resist change. So it is our old habits that often resist change. This is why many change models have some kind of initial step which is about challenging, discomforting or 'unfreezing' our old habits, making us 'conscious' of our incompetence, before moving on to positive change.

For example a popular model is this one developed by Kurt Lewin over sixty years ago:

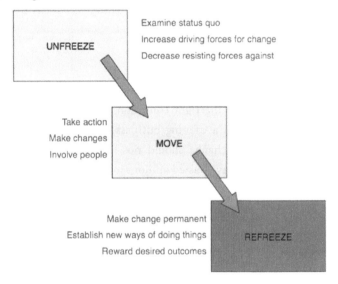

Figure 7 : Kurt Lewin's Model

Lewin's[8] model has endured because it is simple, yet powerful. It recognises a fundamental aspect of the way we are all wired.

---

8   *Resolving Social Conflicts / Field Theory in Social Science* (American Psychological Association; Reprinted edition, 1997)

So there is something challenging about habits when we seek to influence people to change the way they do things, and at the same time our goal is to replace them with newer, better habits, returning people to 'unconscious competence' of an improved kind.

Keystone habits

Many of the unproductive practices in your organisation persist, even when you are aware of them, because they are habits. We are reminded to move towards people, about being less focused on our email Inbox, about not doing "Death by PowerPoint" presentations, not looking at our smart phone in meetings, or that the latest project report we are writing is a waste of time. The list is long, if we had time to write it. Yet we still find ourselves doing all these things. Why?

> The brain is a wonderful organ. It starts working the moment you get up in the morning and does not stop until you get into the office.
>
> **—Robert Frost**

One of my personal previously-unconscious habits is, I have come to realise, to leap to providing the right education as a solution. This is to be expected, perhaps: I do lead a training business. However, there is growing research to show that any change should not be led merely by providing information. Governments have wasted millions in trying to persuade people to eat better, save more, and drink less. Many of these initiatives are clearly wasted because there is little evidence that people adopted new lifestyles or bought the new products in response to these campaigns. The problem isn't one of lack of information. On the contrary, it's about what you do when you are not thinking about it.

Perhaps the solution is simpler and stronger than you think; as simple as addressing or replacing the habits that inhibit you.

> Faced with the choice between changing one's mind and proving that there is no need to do so, almost everyone gets busy with the proof.
>
> **— J. K. Galbraith**

In *The Power of Habit*[9], Charles Duhigg references a study where it was "found more than 40 percent of the actions people performed each day weren't actual decisions, but habits." Further he argues that habits "shape our lives far more than we realize – they are so strong, in fact, that they cause our brains to cling to them at the exclusion of all else, including common sense."

Daniel Kahneman[10] explains this from neurology. Basically our brains follow the path of least resistance:

> "…if there are several ways of achieving the same goal, people will eventually gravitate to the least demanding course of action. In the economy of action, effort is a cost, and the acquisition of skill is driven by the balance of benefits and costs. Laziness is built deep into our nature."

New connections between the synapses of the brain are weak and temporary - electrostatic. But with practice (repetition), these connections morph into more permanent biochemical links. Less effort is required to navigate through them. So changing a habit means working against some pretty 'hard-wired' pathways in your brain. We all have a natural aversion to this.

Now, I'm sure that the previous paragraph doesn't inspire you, does it? However, there are some encouraging findings from this line of research. Duhigg quotes someone who specialises in helping people reverse habits:

> "…once you're aware of how your habit works, once you recognize the cues and rewards, you're halfway to changing it… It seems like it should be more complex. The truth is, the brain can be reprogrammed. You just have to be deliberate about it."

Can it really be as simple as it sounds?

> Chip and Dan Heath[11] wrote about research run by the Cornell University Food and Brand Lab. In the study, movie goers were given, for free, medium and large buckets of popcorn. Both buckets were too big for

9   Random House, 2013.
10   *Thinking, Fast and Slow* (Penguin, 2012).
11   *Switch: How to change things when change is hard*
(Random House Business: 2011).

individuals to finish and the popcorn was stale (one movie goer compared it to "styrofoam packing peanuts") so that people weren't eating it for pleasure. Yet people with the larger buckets ate 53% more popcorn.

They re-ran many variations of the experiment and each time the results were the same: "People eat more when you give them a bigger container. Period."

The lesson from this is that often it's just easier to change the size of the container than to try to teach people to think differently about food. This does open up new possibilities in leading people through change.

Duhigg explores what he calls "Keystone Habits", habits that have the amazing ability to dramatically affect many other habits in your life. Here is how he described them:

"The habits that matter most are the ones that, when they start to shift, dislodge and remake other patterns… Keystone habits say that success doesn't depend on getting every single thing right, but instead relies on identifying a few key priorities and fashioning them into powerful levers…If you focus on changing or cultivating keystone habits, you can cause widespread shifts."

For example, one of my keystone habits, I have come to realise, is journaling. I frequently keep a journal simply as a means of self-reflection and developing my self-awareness, a key emotional intelligence.

One of the implications of all this is that part of understanding your stakeholders is to see as well as to listen. What practices do you see? Are there clues as to what we might identify as target 'keystone habits'?

Sometimes, unthinking habits can make a consultant look good:

A number of years ago, I was once asked for advice on a problem by a team leader whose function it was to validate and clean data for classified advertising. She shared this function with the leader of another team. They both covered complementary regions across the

UK. The problem was workload management. Each morning, the raw data arrived in the form of a stack of continuous computer listing paper. When the team leaders divided the stack up by region, it was usually obvious that one team had disproportionately more work to do that day than the other team.

I asked why they didn't just split the list in half each day. I merely asked this for clarification, assuming that there must have been a good reason.

My client looked thunderstruck with my apparent genius. "That's brilliant. Thank you very much!" From then on the two teams just split the stack each day.

4. Recognise and minimise the pain of change

Leaders who recognise the pain involved in change, seek to minimise that pain, and when they are seen to minimise it, they are more influential as a result. Closely allied with the first principle, this empathy builds to the point where people feel they are working on a difficult challenge shoulder-to-shoulder with the change leader. If you are familiar with risk management you might like to think of the potential pain you could cause others as a risk.

Psychologists tell us that the pleasure-pain principle is a major driver in human behaviour. We are pain-minimisers: we are constantly seeking strategies to minimise the pain in our lives, whether we are aware of it or not. As a consequence, if someone comes our way and reduces the pain in our lives, then we gravitate towards them. This is a powerful influencing strategy.

So the perceived pain in other people's lives, both in their current state and the change we seek to take them through, should be something we take note of, something in our frame of reference.

We will explore a number of techniques that will help live this principle.

5. High performance comes through people and action

Choose a path and execute like hell.

— Jack Welch

This is a principle about our own internal attitudes.

Growing evidence is available that people who make better leaders always have a leaning to action. They are never victims of 'paralysis by analysis'. Research by Professor Len Schlesinger[12] and others shows that entrepreneurs are always taking cautious next steps - not recklessly, but with considered risks. Similarly, Stephen Covey[13] identified highly successful people as having a distinctive pro-active habit. They lean into life and make things happen.

As well as a leaning to action, our research has shown that high performing project and programme managers all have a leaning to relationships. We found that high performers all had a far higher proportion of their discretionary time devoted to engaging with other people, quite apart from the structured meetings and emails that we normally describe as 'communicating.' They just spend more time moving towards, and talking with, people.

Hence the Value Ladder considered earlier is supported both by a leaning to people and action.

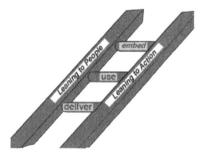

---

12   *Just Start: Take Action, Embrace Uncertainty, Create the Future*, co-authored with Charles Keifer, (Harvard Business Press: 2012).
13   *The 7 Habits of Highly Effective People* (Simon & Schuster: 2004)

Changing the metaphor, you could also compare this principle to a bicycle (Figure 8). The front wheel gives direction; this is the leaning to relationships. The rear wheel gives the drive; it is the leaning to action.

Figure 8 : The engagement bicycle

6. Integrity is powerfully persuasive

If you can fake integrity you've got it made.

(Hollywood graffiti)

Of course, you can't fake integrity; that's an oxymoron. Instead, if you operate out of internal integrity, people learn to trust what you say and the commitments you make to them.

The pay-off of walking with integrity is huge, and long-term. You may find yourself in new contexts, where your stakeholders are used to being treated with duplicity and deceit. It may take a while, and some courage, before people start to believe you and trust you. Your reputation for integrity, though, is gained in those moments where it is difficult. These are the defining moments, where the temptation to lie is strong. If you have the courage of your convictions, people around you will notice. Believe me, they will notice.

There is no substitute for leading with integrity. Yet many seem to try.

At some point in your life you must decide whether you
want to impress people or influence people. You can
impress people from a distance, but you must get close
to influence them, and when you do that, they will be
able to see your flaws. That's okay. The most essential
quality for leadership is not perfection, but credibility.
People must be able to trust you, or they won't follow
you.

Rick Warren

Trust is the bandwidth of communications.

—Karl-Erik Sveiby

As Warren shows, there is a close relationship between integrity and trust.
Guy Kawasaki[14] provides a very helpful checklist on trustworthiness:

- Trust others first. Give people the benefit of the doubt. Risks are
  more than outweighed by the benefits to you.

- Under-promise and over-deliver.

- Deliver bad news early.

- Have an abundant mindset, rather than a scarcity mindset (where
  everything is a zero-sum game).

- Tell people what you don't know.

- Figure out what you don't know, and then find out and provide
  the answer.

- Disclose your interests. If you have a conflict of interest, tell people.

---

14   *Reality Check* (Penguin, 2008).

7. Feelings trump reason & meaning trumps authority

At first glance, the world of business appears to be a rational enterprise. We are children of the enlightenment, where we expect the world, and the people within it, to behave rationally. I find all too many management books are written with this presupposition.

But it turns out that this is not the reality within which we actually work.

Professor John Kotter of Harvard illustrates how powerful emotions are in the arena of change. We have been taught to put reasonable propositions to people. We present our reasoned business cases, plans, and reports, and so we expect people to think on them and then act. Kotter[15] says the expected sequence is:

Reason - Analyse - Act

Almost always the real sequence is more like this:

See - Feel - Act

It seems we are not the rational beings we thought we were, no matter how sophisticated the lifestyles we live[16]. It appears that people engage with their stakeholders better if there is some kind of emotional connection. For example, don't we find that when it comes to public speaking we would all prefer to listen to people who present with genuine passion than those who merely read out papers or bullet lists?

Marketing professionals understand this. As an experiment, analyse several TV commercials. Are the advertisements about the specifications and features of the products and services they are selling? Or are they more to do with exciting certain emotions, or conveying the kind of person you would be if you used their products?

---

15   *The Heart of Change: Real-Life Stories of How People Change their Organizations*, co-authored with Dan S. Cohen, (Harvard Business Review Press: 2002).
16   See Viktor Frankl's unique autobiography in, *Man's Search for Meaning: The classic tribute to hope from the Holocaust* (Rider: 2004) and Daniel Pink's, *Drive*, op cit.

Also, it appears that in seeking to influence people, we should have more regard to the reasons rather than the features. The meaning of what people do, and connecting them to it, can become a powerful motivator.

Further, we have historically placed high value in the authority that comes with organisational hierarchy. In many organisations this can be somewhat deceptive. All too often power does not operate as a simple aggregation of where people sit in the hierarchy. Nor is power evenly distributed. We find that real power does not map onto the organisational chart exactly. Moreover, we often find people work in areas where they have little or no understanding of why they are doing certain jobs; they continue them out of some sort of obedience to tradition. So introducing an explanation of 'why' people should change to certain practices can be more powerfully motivating than command-and-control styles of management that do not care to provide reasons.

Am I suggesting that you should abandon logic and authority structures? Not at all. Clearly we need to make rational sense, particularly to certain stakeholders. Our numbers need to add up, and there needs to be a logical sequence to the way we set things out. But we have overemphasised rationality in traditional management to the exclusion of all else. The point of this principle is the reality that there are more powerful forces at work sometimes in the realm of emotions, affections and meaning. In order to influence effectively, we need to recognise these and work with them.

Living the principles

You will find towards the end of the following chapters a section that discusses how you might live or express each of the principles.

Use these seven principles as a daily reminder all the way through your engagement with people.

Principles - Summary

- These principles are compass points in the sometimes-chaotic world of change, dealing with people of all kinds. We have found them to be universal, self-validating and empowering

- Use them as a daily reminder:

  » Seek first to understand ... then be understood

  » Effective change is always led

  » Habits are the inhibitors and the goal

  » Recognise and minimise the pain of change

  » High performance comes through people and action

  » Integrity is powerfully persuasive

  » Feelings trump reason and meaning trumps authority.

Themes

> It is well to remember that the entire universe, with
> one trifling exception, is composed of others.
> **—John Andrew Holmes**

This section surfaces some of the major themes that run throughout the engagement pathway.

Themes are not principles and do not sit well within any one step on the pathway. Hence they are separated out for particular consideration.

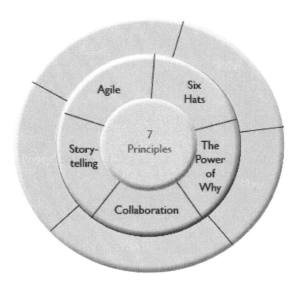

CHAPTER 4

The six engagement hats

I have opinions of my own -- strong opinions
-- but I don't always agree with them.

— George Bush

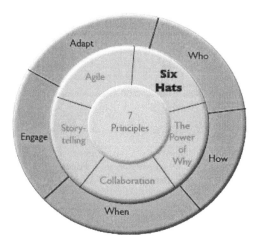

P eople, as we have noted, are complex. Taking a single perspective on a stakeholder in order to understand and influence them is likely to miss important clues. So it is better to take a more rounded approach, taking several complementary perspectives on a person or group.

Edward de Bono developed the Six Thinking Hats technique[1] for problem solving and creativity. Similarly, we can conceive of at least six "hats" or perspectives that can add value to our attempts to understand and engage people.

---

1   *Six Thinking Hats*, (Penguin: 2009).

These are:

- The marketer

- The change agent

- The politician

- The accountant

- The leader

- The speculator.

Each of these hats has particular merit; each has insights into stakeholders that the other perspectives might overlook. In the following sections we explore the perspectives of each hat and the questions they bring to stakeholder engagement.

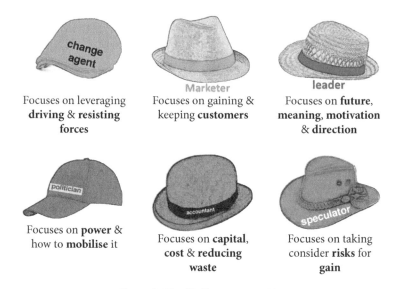

Focuses on leveraging **driving** & **resisting** **forces**

Focuses on gaining & keeping **customers**

Focuses on **future**, **meaning, motivation** & **direction**

Focuses on **power** & how to **mobilise** it

Focuses on **capital**, **cost** & **reducing** **waste**

Focuses on taking consider **risks** for **gain**

Figure 9 : The Six Engagement Hats

Thinking like a marketer

Marketer

Business has only two functions –
Marketing and innovation.

—Peter F. Drucker

Wikipedia defines marketing as "the process of communicating the value of a product or service to customers. It is a critical business function." Many of us in project management, have believed the "Field of Dreams"[2] myth: "Build it, and they will come." Alas, they will not. People do not automatically and enthusiastically use what we deliver; neither do markets automatically buy and consume new products.

You could argue that stakeholder engagement is a form of marketing. Some organisations take this idea seriously enough that they even have internal marketing offices.

Marketing includes so much more than selling. It includes discovering unsatisfied wants, creating a value proposition, pricing that proposition, promoting the product, and ensuring that there are adequate distribution systems to satisfy the demand for that value that has been aroused.

The marketer focuses on potential **customers**, and how to **gain** and **keep** them. They think about who the target customer is, how to make a product **visible and attractive** to them, and what sort of **message** and advertising would make the target customer want to buy.

Thus we have much to learn from the field of marketing. It contains a rich body of work about influencing people to act, and so is deeply relevant to how we engage with our stakeholders.

When wearing the marketer hat ask yourself:

- Who is my customer? Who is a potential customer?

- What are their unsatisfied wants?

- How could I meet those wants?

- How can I keep that customer satisfied?

---

2 A 1989 Movie starring Kevin Costner (Universal Pictures) where the hero hears a voice that whispers. "Build it and they will come."

Thinking like a change agent

You're gonna need a bigger boat.

—Chief Martin Brody[3]

A change agent is someone who seeks to take people through some sort of **transition**, usually as a colleague or a peer. A change agent tends to follow some kind of **change management model** in navigating themselves and others through change.

The change agent focuses on the **drivers** and **resistors** to change, and how they can work with these. The change agent is mindful of the difficult transitions from **old to new habits** of behaviour that people must make in order to get the best outcome possible. The change agent looks closely at behaviours as a measure of transition to the new.

When wearing the change agent hat ask yourself:

- What are the unconscious habits of the people? What are the irrelevant or irrational habits? What are the 'dead bodies' they walk over?

- What forces (fears and interests) are keeping them where they are?

- How could I weaken those forces?

- What are the drivers for change?

- How can I create a sense of urgency for the change? Is there sufficient momentum or 'felt need' for people to exert themselves to change?

- Which change models would be most appropriate for this organisation?

---

3   From the screenplay of "Jaws", Universal Pictures, 1975.

Thinking like a politician

I have a fantasy where Ted Turner is elected president but refuses because he doesn't want to give up power.

—Arthur C. Clark

The politician will look for where **power** lies. This is not always all at the top of an organisation and not always in formal structures. The politician will gain **powerful allies** and seek to build a **coalition of powerful people** behind their change **agenda**. The politician seeks to mobilise that **power** for their agenda.

The politician will also be looking out for **early victories** and using these to good effect in their communications with other stakeholders.

You may not like the world of politics and believe that people should not be 'political' in business, but the truth is that power is distributed unequally in organisations, and those who learn where power is, how it works, and how to mobilise it, are often more effective in getting their changes through. People in organisations are political, so we do need some political awareness in order influence effectively.

When wearing the politician's hat, ask yourself:

- Where does the real power lie?

- Do I have sufficiently powerful people backing my agenda?

- How can I mobilise more power behind my change?

- Are there other competing/conflicting agendas?

- Are there success stories I can tell that will rally people to my cause?

- Where do I need to negotiate?

Thinking like an accountant

Today will never happen again. Don't waste it with a false start or no start at all.

—Og Mandino

The accountant works in numbers, in measurement. This perspective can add clarity, credibility, and urgency, as well as add appropriate rigour that may be lacking in the other perspectives. They look for what can be verified. The accountant focuses on **capital**, the **costs** involved in change, as well as where **waste** can be eliminated. These concepts can be applied to relationships.

The accountant sees valuable relational **capital**, or lack of it, in each stakeholder relationship. The common idiom in the West when someone responds to a favour – "I owe you one" – hints at this concept. The engagement pathway can be viewed as a series of transactions, seeking to avoid going into relational 'deficit.'

The accountant also focuses on **cost**. 'Cost' here might be the pain of change, and they will seek to minimise it. The accountant is also alert to **waste**. Waste can appear in the way an organisation currently operates, with unnecessary steps in a process or inefficient use of resources. When waste is identified and priced, it can become quite clarifying for other stakeholders and help them to see the urgent need to eliminate it. A focus on waste and the quest to eliminate it is helpful, both in the current state of things as well as in the change itself.

When wearing the accountant's hat ask yourself:

- What can I measure about where we are now?

- Where is waste in the current system?

- Where are the potential losses in the change? Where are the potential gains? What is the net gain for each stakeholder? Is it positive or negative?

- Is there sufficient capital invested in the relationships that matter? How can I deposit more?

- How will I be able to tell that we have succeeded?

Thinking like a leader

leader

> Leadership is the ability to see reality as it really is
> and to mobilise the appropriate response.
>
> **—Noel Tichy**

Leaders deal in the currency of **meaning** and are concerned with **direction**. They ask and attempt to offer answers to the '**Why**' question. Through communicating meaning and a better future, they seek to **motivate** those they seek to lead.

Leaders are focused on the tension between a less-than-satisfactory present and the desired future. They typically inhabit that uncomfortable space between what is and what should be. They gain clarity of some beneficial future and build in tension between the current state and that future by communicating the difference. Leaders hold up a mirror to people and show them how things could be.

The most effective leaders lead by example; they model the change they are seeking to bring into reality. Also they work with others, they collaborate, they work with teams. Leading often means making oneself vulnerable, to stand up and stand out for change.

When wearing the leader's hat, ask yourself:

- Why are we doing this? So what?

- What is in it for each stakeholder?

- How can I connect with this person's motivation?

- How can I clarify the future goal? How can I contrast it with where we are now?

- How can I lead by example?

- How can I create clear and compelling messages?

Thinking like a speculator

> If you wait to do everything until you're sure it's right,
> you'll probably never do much of anything.
>
> **—Win Borden**

Speculators deal in probabilities of **risk**, both threats and opportunities. They focus on taking considered risk for **gain**. Considered in this way, we are considering something professional and dynamic. We are not treating stakeholder engagement as a topic in isolation from other areas of enterprise, such as risk management. This perspective helps us to remain risk aware, looking at different alternatives in terms of different risk mixes. The speculator's perspective helps you lean into action.

Major changes, programmes and projects have risk registers. There is a relationship between each risk and your stakeholders. Stakeholders are the scouts for both opportunities and threats - they can provide you with valuable early warning - as well as being the owners of risk, and the victims or beneficiaries of risk.

Also, entrepreneurial behaviour is about taking considered risks.

When wearing the speculator's hat, ask yourself:

- Do I have clarity on the reward, the gain?

- Am I taking enough risk with (this) stakeholder(s)?

- Am I taking too many risks with (this) stakeholder(s)?

- Where are the risks from the stakeholders?

- What should our risk appetite be right now in the change?

- What should our risk appetite be with this stakeholder?

- How can I encourage more appropriate risk-taking from this stakeholder?

Pulling the six perspectives together

So each hat represents a distinctly different perspective on engagement, how you might approach and attack it, and how you might shape it.

The perspectives are complementary, each adding a richer, more rounded view to the others than any one of them individually. They are not alternatives.

Throughout the rest of this book, the dominant perspective is labelled against each Practice or Technique to indicate which is the main perspective used. For example, in the following example, the Change Agent is indicated as the dominant perspective..

Technique: Six hats role-play [Change Agent]

Throughout the engagement pathway:

- Gather your team together and get different people to "wear" the different hats,

- Come at particular challenges of engagement with each person role-playing their hat. To help you do this, use the questions for each hat against current context.

Doing this helps identify both key insights about stakeholders and also better influencing strategies. In this way more robust and well-rounded approaches emerge.

Living the principles through the six hats

All the perspectives the six hats bring add something to living each of the principles. Here are comments on particular hats coming through to express each principle.

Seek first to understand, and then be understood: Taking the broader view of your work is people-centric. This is bound to develop a deeper curiosity about where your stakeholders are coming from, and how best you can engage with them. Marketers by professional intent are curious about people. Leaders qualify themselves by being able to influence and be clearly understood.

Effective change is always led: This is the Leader's perspective, but the other five hats each have contributions. The speculator adds dynamism.

Habits are the inhibitors and the goal: The main perspective that is conscious of this is the change agent, but the accountant also considers unwanted habits as a source of waste.

Recognise and minimise the pain of change: The speculator is interested in pain as well as gain. The accountant can make pain obvious in terms of current waste, as well as measuring the pain of change.

High performance comes through people and action: The politician is well aware of mobilising powerful people to overcome inertia and resistance. The speculator always has a leaning to action.

Integrity is powerfully persuasive: The leader will be aware that they need to model change. The marketer is aware of delivering on promises and that market penetration only gains traction with early customer success. The change agent will seek to maintain integrity as a means of raising trust, as well as reducing resistance to the change.

Feelings trump reason, and meaning trumps authority: The marketer is comfortable with attending to the emotional appeal of a value proposition to people. The leader will lead from wherever they are in an organisation. The politician recognises that power does not always reside at the top, and has to persuade through mutual interests.

Six hats - Summary

So let's summarise the key points of the six hats theme.

- There is more than one way of looking at the business of engaging people. We are likely to be more robust in our approach if we consider multiple perspectives:

    » The marketer

    » The change agent

    » The politician

    » The accountant

    » The leader

    » The speculator.

- The six hats are prime engagement perspectives, but not the only ones.

Six hats Technique

- Six hats role-play.

CHAPTER 5

The power of Why

Knowing the "why" allows people to see context and grasp the importance of their work, enabling pride of their workmanship.

— W.E. Deming

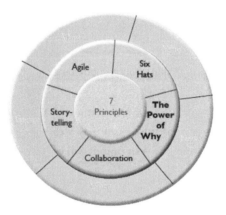

Using the leader's favourite word – 'Why?'

Daniel Pink[1] identifies purpose as a prime motivator for individuals. Viktor Frankl[2] showed that a sense of meaning is crucial to prevailing in tough times and to finding optimal mental health.

Frankl vividly demonstrated this from his own wartime experiences in a death camp. He showed how emotionally healthy it can be to connect with a purpose, a purpose that transcends even the very worst of circumstances. People can deal with almost anything if they have a sufficiently good reason for doing so. Simon Sinek links the power of the "Why" question to trust[3].

---

1   *Drive: the Surprising Truth about What Motivates Us.*
2   *Man's Search for Meaning.*
3   See http://www.youtube.com/watch?v=4VdO7LuoBzM
(viewed September 2013). Also see Sinek's, *Start with Why: How Great Leaders Inspire Everyone to take Action* (Portfolio Penguin, 2009).

To deny people a clear reason for the change they are going through is an abdication of leadership. It amazes me how many people engaged in work do not know why they are doing it. Again and again, research reveals that motivation and performance are significantly enhanced when people can connect with the reason why[4].

Practice: Leading with 'Why?': The key question [Leader]

The 'why' question is powerfully linked with the concept of benefits. Consider again this diagram:

Figure 10 : The relationship of output, outcome, and benefits/goals

Move beyond the 'features' of the output, what you deliver, by asking, "Why does the customer need this?" You may well find that the answer only takes you to a description of how your output will be used, the outcome. So you need to dig deeper and ask a further why or "so what?" This can then uncover the real benefits behind these.

> The things that caused problems for me in school are the same things that help me succeed in the world. I always challenge conventional wisdom. Just because someone says it is so doesn't mean it is so, they have to explain why it is so.
>
> **— Larry Ellison**

Good leaders understand benefits and the power of discovering them, of gossiping them, of exploring them. So be prepared to ask and explain the 'why' frequently in different ways. Use the business case of your change and make sure you and your team can explain its essence, its benefits in language all stakeholders will understand.

---

4   Larson and Lafasto (1991)

Some people can find it quite threatening to be asked "why". It can be threatening because there might be no valid business reason. However, it could be threatening simply in the way we ask it. We can disguise the "why" type of question and make it less challenging, such as: "That's interesting. I'm curious, how did you and your team arrive at the conclusion you needed this?"

I suspect that for some of us, at a very young age, our parents and other authority figures taught us that it is impertinent, perhaps even insolent, to ask why. We need to rediscover the power of asking this question, and its younger sister: "So what?"

> Ask an impertinent question, and you are on your way to getting a pertinent answer.
>
> **—Professor Jacob Bronowski**

Technique: The five whys [Leader]

> He who has a why can bear with almost any how.
>
> **— Viktor Frankl**

Originally developed by Toyota, this technique can be applied to any requirement or problem; with a requirement it helps uncover the end benefits, with a problem it can help uncover the root causes.

It means continuing to dig with the "why" and the "so what" kind of questions, until we uncover the root purpose or driver. Five is simply a guide; sometimes we need to ask it more than that, sometimes less. The key is not to be too easily satisfied with the initial response.

> One of my reviewers told me how he has used the why-what-how hierarchy in his business analysis practice, based on soft systems. It helps people differentiate between the root purpose/driver (why), the focus or primary viewpoint (what) and the options/ choices (how).

Practice: Meaningful marketing [Marketer, Leader]

The people we seek to influence are bombarded with all kinds of demands for their attention. Marketers face the same problem in getting the attention of consumers. Research pulled together by Doug Hall[5] identifies coping habits in consumers who learn to skim through and filter out mindless claims, such as "unsurpassed performance."

Hall encourages sellers to be specific about what they offer, and tell potential customers verifiable differences they will achieve. These he calls meaningful marketing messages, such as "cuts your time in half", the **Overt Benefits**. So he encourages product vendors to be factual and measure the advantage of their offering over the competition. Using words of existing customers to speak about the advantages to them, gives prospective customers a '**Reason to Believe**'. These all contribute to crafting marketing messages that have meaning to people and explain the dramatic difference over what they have now.

This line of analysis converges with the practice of describing measurable benefits. Benefits statements and their plans should be key messages to persuading people in and around the change.

> For example: "Did you know that the process we will use at the end of this will cut the number of complaints to be processed by 60% as measured by the experience of other business units already using it? How would you use that time?"

---

5   *Meaningful Marketing* (Brain Brew Books, 2003), p.50.

Exercise: Create a wall chart with three columns: 'Feature', 'Overt Benefit' and 'Reason to Believe'.

With your team consider what your change will tangibly deliver – your 'product'.

Now list the features of that product down the first column.

In the second column, ask "Why would they want that?: or "So what?". Keep asking these questions until you arrive at a verifiable benefits statement ('Overt Benefit').

In the third column consider what would make your stakeholders believe your claim? Working prototype? Testimonial?

Let the table exercise incubate for a day or two and then return to it. Ask, "Are there pointers here to key messages we need to communicate?"

Living the principles through the power of asking and explaining Why

Seek first to understand and then be understood: At first glance, explaining why seems to apply more to the second half of this principle: being understood. However, at the beginning of an engagement use this question to drive out clarity from your Sponsor.

Effective change is always led: Leadership deals in the currency of meaning, and the question Why works so powerfully because of that.

Habits are the inhibitors and the goal: The why discussions often get behind people's habits. Getting them to explain reasons often removes many of the resisting forces inhibiting them.

Recognise and minimise the pain of change: "He who has a why can bear almost any how." We increase people's sense of purposelessness and therefore pain, if we deny them a clear reason why they need to change. Conversely, where we can clarify the good reasons for the change, it reduces pain.

High performance comes through people and action: People care whether their efforts have significance. Explaining the strategic reasons behind this change does two things: it motivates to performance, and sometimes it empowers others to identify better, simpler, cheaper, faster solutions.

Integrity is powerfully persuasive: People suspect those who are unclear about their reasons. Conversely, being open about the reasons for the change displays integrity of purpose and clarity of thought, and engenders trust.

Feelings trump reason, and meaning trumps authority: Talking about why is the beginning of connecting to feelings. The why gives meaning to the change. Blind authority operates behind the "because I said so" kind of argument. Changing the conversation to talking about the reasons begins to connect with meaning. Talking about valid reasons from strategic intent or internal drivers denies blind authority continuing with meaningless practices, such as pet projects.

Power of Why - Summary

- Seek to connect your stakeholders with the reason for it all, its meaning

- Connecting people with the reasons of why we need to change is motivating and removes much potential resistance

- Take care not to be satisfied with the first "why". There could be deeper reasons underneath it

- Avoid focusing on the features of what you deliver. Instead tease out the benefits through the 'why' and 'so what' questions.

Practices

- Leading with 'why': the key question

- Meaningful marketing.

Technique

- Five whys.

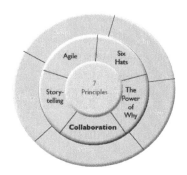

CHAPTER 6
Collaboration

We must all hang together, or assuredly we will all hang separately.

—Benjamin Franklin

Collaboration is one of the most powerful modes of engagement and can speed through all steps in the pathway. Involving appropriate people at appropriate moments with appropriate methods is one of the key tools to high performance engagement.

The immediate group to consider collaborating with is your team; but it doesn't stop there. Let's start with your team, though.

Practice: Lead with your team [Leader]

If you want to go quickly, go alone.
If you want to go far, go together.

—African Proverb

Part of the challenge of giving more time to relationships is just that: time. There never seems to be enough of it. Another is competence: you may not feel you are the most people-oriented person on the planet.

But it needn't all rest on your shoulders. In fact, take a step back a moment. Why do the high performers have such a relational leaning? These people appreciate more clearly than most of us that a project is essentially a social enterprise, a social vehicle of change. It needs a team to scale. It is beyond one person. Our high performers leveraged relationships to get more done through others.

Having identified some of your stakeholders, their interests, their concerns, and their power, it may be obvious that you are not the best person to influence some of them. It might be a matter of your position, your level of seniority, your lack of experience, a lack of common interest, or just a lack of personal chemistry. So you need to ask, "Who *would* be the best person to engage with them?"

For example, suppose there is a particular director in your client organisation that is very impatient with you and antagonistic towards your agenda. What can you do? In these situations it is good to remind yourself that you are part of a wider team. It could well be that you agree with your project executive or another board member (e.g. a PRINCE2 Senior User role on the project board) that they are the ones who will lead on this relationship.

So use your team. Share the burden of engaging with all your stakeholders and servicing these relationships. However, you must be clear who is the lead on each relationship, how they will do it, and how you will be kept informed. And when it comes to clarity in teams, nothing beats writing it down in a common team document.

This is sometimes part of what is called the Stakeholder Engagement Strategy[1].

---

1   See the How Step.

Technique: Assessing team effectiveness [Leader]

During the course of engaging with people, we engage with them as teams. We even find ourselves leading such teams. It matters to the overall success of our engagement that our team performs well.

In fact, with the notable exception of Agile approaches such as Scrum and DSDM, the team is a rather neglected vehicle for delivering change: the literature tends to focus on the individual Hero (e.g. the project manager) or the organisation as a whole. Yet, there is a growing body of evidence that suggests that high-performing teams bring about more change than any one of us. For example, see Professor Lynda Gratton's excellent, *Hot Spots: Why some companies buzz with energy and innovation - and others don't*[2].

So how do we ensure they are working to an optimal level?

Rollin and Christine Glaser[3] distilled this into a simple 5-factor model:

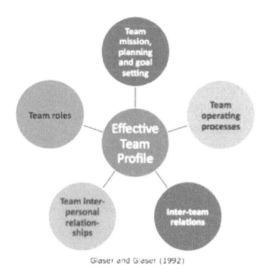

Glaser and Glaser (1992)

Figure 11 : The Glaser and Glaser Model of Team Effectiveness

---

2   Financial Times Prentice Hall, 2007.
3   Glaser, R and Glaser, C, *Team Effectiveness Profile*, (King of Prussia, PA, 1992)

Team mission, planning and goal setting: A number of sources agree that where teams are involved less in routine and more in uncertain change, goal setting becomes even more important. Goals offset some of the negative effects of uncertainty.

So it seems obvious that working with the team to clarify its goals is a crucial priority.

Team Roles: It is quite normal when a team is formed, where some may have never worked together before, for there to be uncertainty around what is expected of each person in the team. However, a team moves more quickly to fluent working if team roles are first clarified. This is not just a case of each person understanding their own role; understanding the roles of all the other team members is also crucial. Every team member should be able to say, "I know what is expected of me, and I know what everybody else is responsible for."

Whenever change happens within a team, or through the work of the team itself, then clarity on roles helps do two things:

1.   It provides everyone with a clear sense of purpose.

2.   It provides a supportive framework for tasks to be completed.

Of course, there is a balance to be struck here. Too much rigidity in roles might be unhelpful in very dynamic and fluid situations. There needs sometimes to be a space for innovation, courage, and team members covering for each other. A good team leader reads this carefully.

Team operating process: Before engaging with the enemy in battle, troops need to be clear on their "rules of engagement". This is true even in non-military contexts. Once work begins, where different team members work with other individuals outside of the team, chaos becomes a real threat, where people work at cross-purposes. For example, consider the classic case of one software engineer changing a piece of code at the same time as another team member.

The best teams understand and follow consistently certain operating practices, even if these are more adaptive, such as with the Agile team's retrospectives[4]. Teams formed of individuals who have never worked with each other before need to put particular effort into this; there is no past history to call

---

4   A retrospective is a review meeting at the end of an iteration or sprint, in Agile development. See also the Daily Stand-Up in the Adapt Chapter.

upon, no habits of team working that have yet been formed. All teams do not work the same way. There are a great variety of ways in which teams could work, so the leader needs to get explicit understanding and agreement on the team's way of working.

Team Inter-Personal Relationships: Personality conflicts are common in teams, but they are not a necessary part of team working. Where personality conflicts arise - conflicts not about opinions but about persons - the leader needs to address them quickly, before they become damaging to the team.

The means is through communication, the creation of a transparent, high-trust, no 'elephants in the room' team culture. When the pressure is on the team, for example, to meet a deadline, then the aspect that suffers is relationships within the team - and conflict can ensue.

How does the team leader prevent or prepare for that?

Some approaches to consider are for a leader to co-create with the team a 'team charter' or agree with the team rules of etiquette right at the start. These can become sort of team values, by which everyone is expected to live.

Inter-team relations: No team exists in isolation - just as ticket stubs sometimes say: "Not good if detached." One of the greatest risks to the effectiveness of a team is not always obvious: the team becomes detached from its wider working environment. Those outside of the team, particularly more senior people, can begin to lose a sense of value in the team, and begin to think of it as a self-serving clique[5].

Is individual management competence a false trail?

Allow me to be even more heretical for a moment.

Some excellent work has been done on analysing, measuring and developing individual competences in the field of management. In project management I think of:

- The APM Competence Framework. This is a commendably comprehensive piece of work with clear definitions and measures of maturity.

- SfIA (Skills for the Information Age).

---

5   Barry Oshry's analysis (How Step) is helpful here.

- Cranfield's phenomenological study on programme managers' conceptions of the job.

- The various professional qualifications such as PMP[6], PRINCE2[7], Agile PM[8] and APMP[9], where there are degrees of challenge accrediting an individual's abilities along some scale.

Most of this work starts with the basic assumption that the key to a project's success is the competence of the individual project manager.

But what if this were not true? What if a project's success was predicated more on the performance of the team, a co-operative and fluent team-working, where within that team the project manager was just one role, albeit a pivotal one? In that case, scaling through your team becomes a priority.

We have seen many studies focused on the individual project manager, or on the organisation, but few focusing on the team and its wider community of stakeholders.

Could it be that in their leaning to relationships the high performers lead by example, and model good team behaviours, minimise confusion, and so on? Perhaps in this instance, the individual "competence" mobilises *group competence*, and that it is really the *team* and its wider stakeholders that together get results.

I wonder if the exclusive focus on the individual project manager's competence is another instance of what we discussed in Chapter 1: looking in the wrong places. I suggest that it might be the high performing team that makes the individual look good.

6   See http://www.pmi.org/Certification/Project-Management-Professional-PMP.aspx .
7   Owned by AXELOS Limited.
8   See http://dsdm.org/get-educated as well as http://www.apmg-international.com for Agile PM.
9   See http://www.apm.org.uk/APMQualifications for this and other qualifications by the Association for Project Management.-

Beyond your team

> A client providing a global roll-out of upgraded desktop systems to country offices recently told me about an issue that arose among some country managers who wanted to be earlier in the roll-out schedule.
>
> He gathered these managers together, explained his constraints, and then stepped back to observe their discussion.
>
> After a period of time, the tone of the discussion changed markedly, from self-interested lobbying to deferring to each other on objective merits. In the end they offered him a roll-out sequence to his constraints that everyone had agreed.
>
> It seems that they were much more positive when they knew they were being consulted and began to appreciate each other's issues.

Involving any stakeholder outside your immediate circle of management attracts a number of risks. They might slow you down, seek to shape things to suit themselves, they take the "wrong" decisions, give you a distorted view, try to sabotage your change from the inside, and so on. However, there is a place for considered risk-taking by selectively including stakeholders at key moments[10]. As the short account above shows, involving a wider group in a collaborative manner can speed matters up rather than slow you down. It can resolve problems rather than create them.

Other collaborative techniques

Such is the power of collaboration for getting people to buy-in to your goal, and to get them to align to your cause, that there are quite a number of techniques that have been developed exploiting the power of participation.

Here are some specific examples of collaborative techniques. This is not an exhaustive list, but rather is illustrative.

---

10   *Thinking like a speculator*, in the Six Hats Chapter.

Technique: World Café [Change Agent]

World Café is an approach to facilitating structured conversations among groups[11]. It is a way of keeping conversations focused, but where everyone has a chance to participate. Emergent solutions and themes can often provide breakthrough solutions as well as greater buy-in from the people participating.

There are a number of variations but an approach I use is as follows:

1.   Prepare a large room with round tables each seating about four people. Place a white paper tablecloth on each table.

2.   Brief a sub-group of table facilitators, one per table. They are to record the conversations at their table, if possible graphically with diagrams, cartoons and pictures. Provide them with coloured pens or crayons for this.

3.   Give the group a key question to explore. Have this question displayed prominently somewhere in the room.

4.   The first round lasts about 20 minutes with everyone seated at a table. The facilitator records as much of the table conversation as they can, ensuring also that all have a chance to speak.

5.   At the end of the first round everyone except the facilitators leave their tables. The three leaving any one table must separate to go to other tables.

6.   Round two begins with a new group of people around each table, and the facilitator on each table brings the new group up to speed on the notes in front of them.

7.   The conversations build on these for the rest of round two, ending after a total of twenty minutes.

8.   Repeat 4 to 7 for Round three.

9.   After three rounds call on the facilitators to present back to the groups the notes displayed on a gallery.

10.   Ask the group to identify any emerging themes.

---

11   See www.theworldcafe.com

I attended a leadership conference in Chicago – the Willow Creek Leadership Summit - with about 18 other leaders from the UK. The conference was rich and stimulating, but at moments it was understandably very US-centric.

I was asked to facilitate a wash-up session a couple of days after the conference. So I took the group through the World Café process above. I had prepared four tables and briefed four table facilitators.

Figure 12 : Leadership Summit World Cafe: Table Facilitator presents back

The operating question I used was, "What lessons from the conference will survive the trip home?"

The energy level that morning was high, we were all engaged and intrigued about the outcome. In the end, the wall charts/gallery were preserved and taken back by the leader of our group. Emergent themes did surface, with a stronger consensus on some issues than we all suspected from a fairly diverse group, with some overtly divergent agendas. (See .)

The feedback was that it did build on the conference experience, and helped everybody contextualise the conference material for their situations back home.

The World Café process is particularly useful in the following situations:

- Engaging people - whether they are meeting for the first time, or are in established relationships - in authentic conversation

- Conducting an in-depth exploration of key strategic challenges or opportunities

- Deepening relationships and mutual ownership of outcomes in an existing group

- Creating meaningful interaction between a speaker and the audience

- Engaging groups larger than 12 (World Café have had up to 1200) in an authentic dialogue process.

The Café is less useful when:

- You are driving toward an already determined solution or answer

- You want to convey only one-way information

- You are making detailed implementation plans

- You have fewer than 12 people, in which case it is better to use a more traditional dialogue circle, council or other approach for fostering authentic conversation.

Technique: Knowledge Café [Change Agent]

This is a variant of the World Café used by David Gurteen[12]. David works in the field of knowledge management and mobilisation. The Knowledge Café takes a keynote subject matter expert who is asked to speak for no more than twenty minutes. Then the table groups pick up the key issue or question and make observations that are recorded by a facilitator.

In plenary session the facilitators each feedback the views and ideas of the table, leading to an open conversation, which is usually facilitated by someone other than the initial speaker.

This does allow for rapid knowledge mobilisation, as well as for taking the temperature among stakeholders of a new idea.

A knowledge café could be run as a brown bag meeting over a lunchtime.

Technique: the wiki [Change Agent]

A wiki is a web application that allows participants to enter and edit pages on a web page. The idea has developed, such that parts of cloud-based applications now allow certain objects to behave like wikis.

Think of a wiki as a document that anyone can edit. This allows a degree of collaboration and communication that can be very effective, both in honing messages, as well as the sense of buy-in and energy that comes with that freedom and visibility. Some applications allow changes to be tracked.

Possible applications of a wiki are:

- Group development of text collateral, particularly key messages

- Updating key data on stakeholders

- Sequencing roll-outs and plans

- Priority lists.

Consider who moderates a wiki and how long it should be live. If a document is important enough, someone should be designated with managing and moderating the wiki.

---

12   http://www.gurteen.com/

We used wikis on developing the content and marketing for this book. Using Basecamp[13], I set up a project for the book that eventually included several wiki text documents. Members of the project included my colleagues as well as all the reviewers. Basecamp provided a tracking feature so that we could see who made what changes. (See Figure 13.)

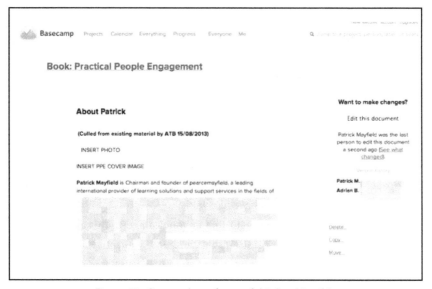

Figure 13 : Screen shot of part of this book's wiki

Note: there is a risk that we reduce collaboration to a matter of which tools or web portals we use. Collaboration is so much more than that; it is primarily about mobilising people's participation rather than merely sharing information and using novel tools. See the Agile Chapter below, and note the first core value in the Agile Manifesto: 'Individuals and interactions over processes and tools.' 14

13   See 37signals.com
14   Chapter 8.

Living the principles through collaboration

Seek first to understand, and then be understood: Collaboration gives stakeholders a voice. For example, the world café allows everyone to have their say. Being understood can be achieved through tools such as the wiki.

Effective change is always led: Collaboration should never be an abdication of leadership, but is often a very potent form of it. Collaboration methods allow you to take the initiative and set the agenda.

Habits are the inhibitors and the goal: Well-executed collaboration mobilises people to participate. Group dynamics in collaboration can often be enough not only to overcome the habits inhibiting change but also to help participants develop healthier new habits in the process. For example, in peer group discussions , people sometimes negotiate: "I will move if I get this." So the individual makes themselves accountable to the group, which helps them deliver on their promises, including developing new habits.

Recognise and minimise the pain of change: Your invitation to a stakeholder to collaborate could in itself be a token of recognition that there is a cost to them. Also, it may remove anxieties about the change happening without them or in a way that does not consult them. The process of collaboration is likely to surface the pain. Collaboration allows stakeholders themselves to suggest solutions that minimise their own pain.

High performance comes through people and action: Asking a group of stakeholders to participate in some collaboration is in itself a means of engaging with them, and by its nature should lead to action. If anything, some collaboration can seem too powerful, sometimes creating a momentum that can be daunting to the change team.

Integrity is powerfully persuasive: What could be more transparent than signaling to a group that you welcome their views and participation? The challenge comes both in setting the boundaries of the collaboration and clearly setting expectations about what you can and can't deliver.

Feelings trump reason, and meaning trumps authority: Participation in these sort of techniques usually generates passion, both positive and negative. This passion is evidence that should be noted just as much as the rational conclusions and recommendations. Moreover, collaboration creates a temporary, artificial governance; within it people can be freed up to explore meaning and give opinions without any of the usual cultural fears and inhibitions. People in session speak more freely on matters that they might be more cautious about in conventional meetings. This again can give you valuable insights about people's real frustrations and hopes.

Collaboration - Summary

- Collaboration begins with your team, but does not end there

- Your team helps you scale engagement, and can make it more effective. Behind every high performer there is probably a high-performing team

- Collaboration is a powerful type of engagement. Anything powerful needs to be used with care

- Collaboration is not simply using a collaborative tool

- Collaboration, well facilitated and well moderated, can be a means to mobilise other stakeholders for your change.

Practices

- Lead with your team.

Techniques

- Assessing team effectiveness with the Glaser & Glaser model

- World Café

- Knowledge Café

- The wiki.

CHAPTER 7

Story-telling

Stories tell us of what we already knew and forgot,
and remind us of what we haven't yet imagined.

—Anne Watson

The human nervous system cannot tell the difference between an
'actual' experience and an experience imagined vividly and in detail.

—Maxwell Maltz

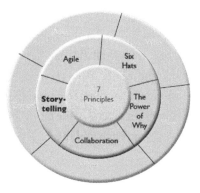

Practice: Leading by story-telling [Leader]

Stories have been a powerful form of conversation since the dawn of humankind. Only recently has story-telling come to be regarded as a legitimate tool within business. Professor Howard Gardner[1] identified storytelling as a strong running theme in all the great twentieth-century leaders he studied.

---

1   *Leading Minds* (Basic Books, reprint 2011).

Some stories are meta-narratives, stories that define an organisation or person or a change. For Martin Luther King it was, "I have a dream."

This becomes important when we realise the power of stories: telling stories transforms people and their perception of the situation. We communicate through stories.

One of the strategic stories that can be compelling when leading a change is the **Creation Narrative** or the **Springboard Story**, as Stephen Denning[2] calls it. It is the story of why an organisation was founded to meet a particular need and conveys the passion that went into setting it up.

A good story[3] has some common elements[4]: a **protagonist** with an initiating incident with a call to action. Note that products are never the protagonist. The protagonist, the Hero, is almost always a person. It usually has a **dreadful alternative** and leads on to the conflict. There is usually a worthy **antagonist**, either external (equal or larger competition) or internal (the opposition to the change). It is important to identify the right antagonist, and this is never a customer (!). Then there is the **transformation**, the change that was achieved, the **resolution of the conflict**, and finally the **moral**. If there's no moral, there's no story, just a succession of facts.

Using a story in this way stands out. With a double-digit growth in the generation of information these days, it is a veritable tsunami of information hitting us. Stories can get through all this storm, can connect with people's imagination, and stick in their minds.

So story-telling is not really another technique, but a rather more pervasive vehicle: the message DNA within several of the techniques mentioned elsewhere in this book, including the Pixar Pitch and the SUCCESs model[5].

We're all story-tellers.

—Jenny Erdal, Ghosting

---

2   *The Leader's Guide to Storytelling: Mastering the art and discipline of business narrative* (Jossey-Bass, 2005).
3   See http://www.youtube.com/watch?v=GQ3BDkMN1LY on corporate storytelling by Doug Stevenson.
4   See Joseph Campbell's *The Hero with a Thousand Faces*, (New World Library, 3rd Ed., 2010).
5   See the How Step Chapter.

Technique: Creating vision statements [Leader]

The very essence of leadership is that you have to have a vision.

—Theodore Hesburgh

A vision describes some beneficial state of things in the future. It can be in the form of a model, a video, a mock-up, but more usually as a vision statement in the form of a short piece of text.

Vision statements have gained a bad press[6]. From what we have seen, most of them deserve that reputation. They are often high-level, vague, and written in such corporate language that their meaning is obscure to many. As a result some have moved away from vision as a leadership tool.

However, it is not so much that vision statements have been tried and found wanting, so much as writing good ones and explaining them adequately have been seen to be too hard and not tried at all.

Yet a well-crafted vision has great power to influence people. The art of writing a good Vision Statement is to think:

1. **End State**: how will the world be different to a customer when your change is finished?

2. **Plain language**: can a ten-year-old understand it? No abstract 'corporate' language please.

3. **Short**: probably shorter than two paragraphs – certainly no longer.

Here is an example vision:

"Imagine when you can access details of your child's progress at school anytime, anywhere, and where you can choose when to be alerted immediately when there is a problem with how well your child is doing."

Note that the vision is about some time in the future. (This one begins with the phrase 'Imagine a time'.) It is describing a future state. It is also written for a wide audience. So it is phrased in non-technical language. And is quite short.

---

6   For example, Cameron and Green (op.cit.) question "Visionary Leadership."

It may not be a vision to everyone's liking (such as the poorly-performing student), but that is not the point; it is clear, and it should appeal to the target stakeholder, in this case parents.

Using a simple story form you can craft one of the most powerful types of vision. Here you consider some individual, some end beneficiary of your change, and write a short story of their future when the benefits flow through.

> I was coaching some postgraduates in the basics of managing their three-year doctoral research as projects. During the introductions, one person, Tom, explained his research in pure jargon. I just about guessed he was a medic researching in the field of cancer, but that was about all I understood.
>
> Later, I led the class through a simple visioning exercise asking them to write a one-paragraph story from the point of view of someone who might benefit from their PhD. This is what Tom wrote:
>
> "I'm a woman with breast cancer. I do not need invasive surgery. Whenever the symptoms present themselves I simply take my medication. It's given me my life back."
>
> This is much clearer and more motivational. It did make an emotional connection with me. I might invest in that research, wouldn't you?

> **Exercise**: Write a one-paragraph vision of the world or your organisation after your change is done.
>
> Give it to someone outside your organisation – a friend, a spouse, or someone else who will give you their honest opinion. Ask them: it is clear? Does it inspire them, if they were to be someone living in that future?

Technique: Customer journey mapping [Marketer, Speculator]

Customer journey mapping is a way of describing as a story all the experiences a customer has in transacting with your organisation and the emotions that are provoked along the way.

It is often the case that, in delivering a service, the customer experience is damaged by one detail in their journey: for example, a junior staff member gives an off-hand or rude response, or a fine-dining restaurant serves a wonderful dish with a dirty fork.

The public sector has taken up this technique in recent years in mapping out its customers' experience, finding it has helped:

- Deal with customers more effectively

- Retain customers

- Increase efficiency

- Minimise negative customer experiences

- Deliver consistently good service.

Fortune magazine says that 85 per cent of dissatisfied customers tell 10 people about their experience, delighted customers tell eight people, and satisfied ones tell five.

With stakeholder empathy at its heart, customer journey mapping helps identify key needs, likes and dislikes, and the current experience of the customer. It helps to plan the best experience for that customer and where communication is at its most appropriate.

Typically a team would work on a map together in this format:

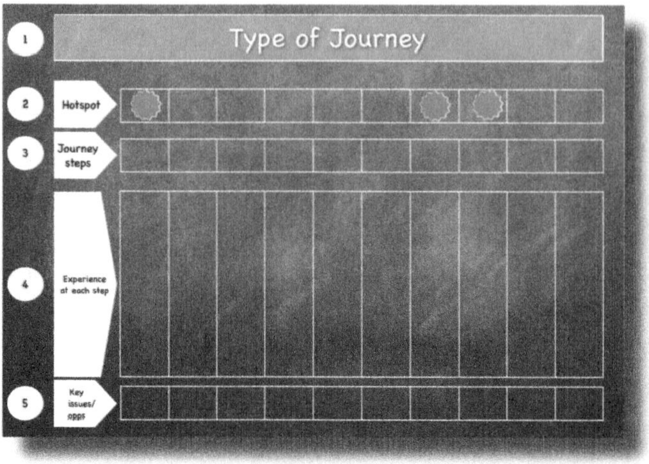

Figure 14 : The template for a Customer Journey Map

The map tells a typical story or journey of a customer through the service from the left hand side to the right. Be specific about the particular journey (1). This journey typically equates to several User Stories[7].

Hotspots (2) are the points of greatest turn in attitude: that is, moments where you can win over a customer or greatly disappoint them. Related to this are **Voting Points**: a key point at which your customer is likely to pause to evaluate if they are delighted, satisfied or dissatisfied with their experience. It is at this point that the customer could 'vote' whether to stay or leave - it is a **key moment of truth**.

The **Journey Steps** row (3) is where you sequence the journey. You should not have too many, and typically you are looking for 3 or 4 'moments of truth' (hotspots). Consider the **touch points**: any point where the customer interacts with your organisation.

The next row (4) maps out the **service actions** that matter to customers at each step – what is likely to deliver the optimum experience for them. **Key issues and opportunities** (5) row is where you and the team agree what should be tackled as a priority.

---

7   See the Agile Theme.

Conclusions are often reached by teams using this technique, such as:

- The customer's experience can improve markedly with timely information

- It is less about functions offered; sometimes the experience improves if there is *less* on offer.

The use of Customer Journey Mapping is not just relevant in a visionary sense – what do we want the ideal customer experience to look like – but also to shape the stakeholder experience *during* your change. You and your team could create a Customer Journey Map as part of the How Step in testing how the cumulative experience of the change plays out for one or more stakeholders ('customers').

Technique: Storyboard your key messages [Leader]

Storyboarding is a technique formalised by Walt Disney, the creator of animated cartoon movies, as way of illustrating stories and developing story ideas. It has since been taken up by creatives of all sort, where they need to sequence some sort of narrative story.

The process of storyboarding is very simple:

1. Brainstorm the elements of your story, using one or more change models.

2. Using large sticky notes[8], rough out a visual representing each step or frame in the change story.

3. Shuffle the sequences if they don't seem right.

4. Append a short-form of the key message behind each frame in the story.

This is all to do with managing expectations and is very important if you don't want to disappoint people unnecessarily, where you need to keep their confidence in your competence.

---

8   I used ArteFact cards from http://shop.smithery.co/ in the illustration. ArteFact Cards come with a Sharpie pen. The size of the cards constrains the graphic and forces you to be visually creative.

For example, if you were to follow Kotter's model[9] your key messages would change throughout the life of your initiative … and afterwards. Behind each frame in the storyboard would be the essence of the key message. These can be placed below each frame using a large sticky note. In this case the messages could be:

1. "We will be in breach of new legislation if we don't change our pension system in a year's time. This could be more than an embarrassment and the cost of a fine. It could lose us key staff and our reputation." (Creating a sense of urgency).

2. "We have the Finance Director leading a trouble-shooting team to make sure we are not just legal but remain progressive." (Building a Powerful Coalition).

3. "Our vision is that we will have a legally-compliant pension system which will not disadvantage the long-term prosperity of our loyal staff." (Creating the vision).

4. "Your line manager will be able to explain what the new pension system will mean for you and how you will work differently when it is in place." (Communicating the vision).

5. "The Edinburgh office has volunteered to pilot the new system." (Empower others to act on the vision).

6. "Edinburgh is so pleased with the new system that they are setting up a series of webinars about their experiences." (Plan for and create short-term wins).

7. "The Edinburgh team has been asked to support Dublin and Cardiff in the second wave of going over to the new system. They have set up a national help desk for all enquiries about this system." (Consolidate improvements and produce still more change).

8. "This year we are setting performance measures based on the pension system we brought in last year." (Institutionalise new approaches).

---

9   See the How Step Chapter.

So you could create a sort of storyboard or sequence of key events, thus:

Figure 15 : The pension scheme as a storyboard

Then, behind each frame, you could attach sticky notes of the key messages appropriate to that frame:

Figure 16 : A frame with its associated messages.

Living the principles by story-telling

Seek first to understand, and the be understood: Story-telling is a potent means of being understood. Part of the power of the story is that you do not need to include everything; the audience is engaged with empathising with the protagonist and making their own specific applications.

Effective change is always led: Denning, Gardner, Pink and others make the case that story-telling is key tool in leading people.

Habits are the inhibitors and the goal: Stories can hold a mirror up to present habits without people feeling accused. They begin to think through future habits as part of the story.

Recognise and minimise the pain of change: Stories can be used to recognise the pain in the crisis or conflict of change, as wel as showing how people win through to the resolution, showing that all the pain is worth it.

High performance comes through people and action: Telling stories is engaging. Stories can be remembered and repeated, so that there is a very short step for the story-teller to begin to live the story. What we vividly imagine is hard for us to distinguish from reality.

Integrity is powerfully persuasive: This principle is important for the way that stories are told, the contexts within which they are told, and what the moral is that the story contains.

Feelings trump reason, and meaning trumps authority: Stories can so grip people that they buy into the proposition without hesitation. Stories play out meaning in all kinds of ways.

Story-telling Summary

- Stories remain as powerful vehicle for conveying messages and story-telling is increasingly recognised as legitimate in business

- A good story has certain key elements

- Clarify your key messages through the story and consider a visual storyboard.

Practice

- Leading by story-telling.

Techniques

- Creating vision statements

- Customer journey mapping

- Storyboarding your key messages.

CHAPTER 8

Agile

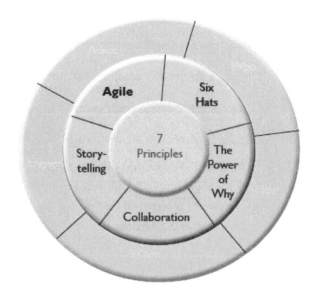

I n what follows, I use the term 'Agile' in a brand sense, embracing a collection of methods, techniques, and approaches, and not the more commonly used adjective.

The adoption of Agile is snowballing. If I were to map Agile project management onto Everett Roger's Innovation Cycle[1], I would say that, at the time of writing, we are moving from the Early Adopters into the Early Majority. Agile is here to stay.

The reason for this is the same reason I've focused on the principles and practices of good people engagement: it works. And so it is not surprising that the Agile practices all share some common strands with the best expressions of people engagement.

The relationship between the best of Agile and stakeholder engagement practice is two-way:

1. Agile works best if it is introduced and supported by good stakeholder engagement.

2. We can learn valuable lessons from what has emerged through Agile practices over the last fifteen years and apply these to the practice of people engagement.

---

1   See the How Step Chapter.

Consider the Agile Manifesto[2] and its four core values:

- **Individuals and interactions over processes and tools.**

- Working software over comprehensive documentation.

- **Customer collaboration over contract negotiation.**

- Responding to change over following a plan.

I've emboldened the first and third as these are immediately congruent with good people engagement, but all four agree with advice in this book. In Scrum, for example, the presence of the Product Owner, the use of User Stories, the release of early working versions, reinforce the practice of staying closely engaged within the developer-customer relationship.

Now consider the Manifesto's twelve principles:

- **Satisfying 'customers' through early and continuous delivery of valuable work.**

- Breaking big work down into smaller components that can be completed quickly.

- Recognising that the best work emerges from self-organising teams.

- **Providing motivated individuals with the environment and support they need and trust them to get the job done.**

- Creating processes that promote sustainable efforts.

- Maintaining a constant pace for completed work.

- Welcoming changing requirements, even late in a project.

- **Assembling the project team and business owners on a daily basis throughout the project.**

- **At regular intervals, having the team reflect upon how to become more effective, then tuning and adjusting behaviour accordingly.**

- Measuring progress by the amount of completed work.

2   Beck, Kent, et al. (2001), "Manifesto for Agile Software Development", Agile Alliance. http://agilemanifesto.org/

- Continually seeking excellence.

- Harnessing change for competitive advantage.

As with the values, a case could be made that all of these principles uphold good people engagement, but I've emboldened the ones that most directly relate to the practices set out in this book.

The overall picture of Agile, even without diving into the detail of the differences between Scrum, DSDM, XP and so on, is that the Agile approach largely works so well because it works with the grain of good people engagement.

What I find fascinating is that many are now finding the adoption of a true Agile development approach to be essentially a cultural challenge, not a technical one. For example, see Brian Wernham's[3] book among others on this. Many of his conclusions about stakeholder engagement and leadership principles apply equally well to the private and not-for-profit sectors as they do to the government sector. Once again, it's a matter of getting the frame of reference right.

If your organisation decides to adopt Agile development of whatever flavour, it will need strong stakeholder engagement as part of that journey.

There are certain Agile practices and techniques that we can usefully exploit for better people engagement. Here, to illustrate this, is one technique and one practice.

---

3   Op. cit.

Technique: User Stories [Leader, Marketer]

User stories are a popular technique commonly used as part of Agile projects. However they can be used for all kinds of change. The technique has grown out of a sense of frustration with the abstraction of written requirement specifications.

A user story has a very simple structure, written in the first person of an operative or user of what will be delivered using this structure:

'As' [user] 'I want to' [goal] 'so that' [reason]

So for example, a user story might read thus:

> 'As a **potential customer**, I want to **have confidence that the people I'm dealing with can be trusted and to know how the shipping of my order is progressing** so that I **might buy more from them later.**'

Often a user story is hand-written, pinned to a board in the development room, written at the beginning of a dialogue with a representative of this stakeholder group, and forming a key part of the conversation. User stories can often begin life as part of a stakeholder workshop.

Writing a user story in the first person seems to make quite an impact. For example, it's been said that the Beatles' song lyrics connected so well with fans because many of them were written in the first person: "I wanna hold your hand." etc.[4] It seems that thinking of ourselves as the stakeholder in the first person begins to connect us with the stakeholder more viscerally, helping us to empathise better with what they want to do and why.

Also, the last part of the User Story syntax is powerful: "So that I can ..." This begins to help the designers and developers conceive of better solutions for that stakeholder. It begins to make the implicit benefits of the request explicit and overt[5].

Think of a user story as complementary to traditional specifications, not as an alternative.

---

4   I recognise this example breaks down somewhat with "I am the Walrus..."
5   See 'Meaningful Marketing' in the Power of Why Chapter.

Some kind of completion test should be agreed with the user or user representative: 'How will we know when we have delivered the sort of experience you want?'

So whether you are clarifying your outcome as a vision statement or as a user story, try it with your internal stakeholders - your project sponsor and/or your team - getting this clarity before testing it further with external stakeholders.

Exercise: Identify three roles, one of which is an external customer, and write a user story from each stakeholder's perspective.

If you are able, show the story to a person representing each of these roles and ask them to comment.

Did they agree and endorse that story for themselves?

Did it help them to articulate what they really wanted, even if their story wasn't quite right?

What are your reflections on the quality of the conversations around these stories? Were they clarifying?

Practice: Self-organising teams [Leader]

This practice is central to the Agile philosophy of development, where a team decides for itself who does what and how. It works where there is some overlap of skills and perspectives, but not so much where all that is generated is group think – that is, the risk of group agreements of the predictable. Consider this example of a self-organising team:

> An organisation approves the idea of an open day for the public. A self-directing team is formed to make this happen. It has to cover a lot of ground very quickly. Time is fixed, and people bring different perspectives to bear on how the open day can be designed, how safety and security is observed by casual visitors, ideas are generated on exhibits and events from different departments, and internal competitions are created to generate a sense of 'buzz' and buy-in through participation. A public marketing plan is developed to coordinate all of these. Decisions are made on access, transport, on-site catering and open hours, by the team.

This kind of scenario illustrates that, where there is a clear mandate of limited scope and urgency, a self-organising team can work well. In creating such self-organising teams:

1.   Agree a clear mandate, that sets broad parameters around the work. Consider using user stories to do this.

2.   Provide clear funding and time constraints.

3.   If possible, provide a team room or safe location, a 'sand pit'. Self-organising teams work best when co-located. Much collaboration happens informally in these rooms.

4.   Carefully select the team in terms of representing different skills, departments, seniority, and experience.

5.   Provide the team protected time away from the normal work.

6. Allow the team to get on in short sprints to develop and deliver solutions, reporting back at agreed dates with agreed working products. Impress that the team must deliver at the end of each sprint.

7. Back off, and do not interfere with the team's decision-making during the sprints or iterations. If necessary, protect the team from interference from others, such as their line managers and other stakeholders with strong opinions. Allow them to surprise you with their creativity[6]. Within a sprint, the team knows best.

Self-organising teams can generate an energy and velocity that can supercharge your change initiative. But it does require clear parameters from the organisation and the protection that goes with that.

Living the principles in the Agile way

Seek first to understand and then be understood: The User Story is a simple but powerful technique to gain understanding from the key stakeholder: your customer. One Agile expert described a User Story as "an excuse for a conversation", an engagement. In Agile understanding both ways is developed empirically by working prototypes.

Effective change is always led: Self-organising teams appear to be leaderless, but looking more closely they actually empower everyone to be leaders. The Daily Stand-Up[7] provides peer group accountability.

Habits are the inhibitors and the goal: All practices are questioned and are open to challenge in the self-directing team. Inherited habits have nowhere to hide. Team members are found to coach each other in new habits, new working practices..

Recognise and minimise the pain of change: Keeping scope and technique as simple as possible is one of Agile's strengths. It minimises the pain of everyone's involvement.

High performance comes through people and action: The drive to deliver tested results at the end of each iteration creates what the Agile people call velocity. Silos of user and developer are broken down to achieve this.

---

6   This is what Wernham calls "Light-Tight" governance.
7   This is an Agile technique we consider in the Adapt Step.

Integrity is powerfully persuasive: Progress is reported on what has been tested and demonstrated to work, not on 'estimates to complete.' Those outside well-run self-directed teams trust what they are told.

Feelings trump reason, and meaning trumps authority: The first person form of the User Story helps the team identify with the user. The 'so that I can' phrase helps them connect with the real meaning and purpose of the requirement.

Agile - Summary

- There is no contention with the Agile Manifesto and the approach of better people engagement. One needs the other

- The User Story and the Self-Organising Team are of value to us in people engagement.

Agile Practice

- The Self-Organising Team.

Agile Technique

- The User Story.

Pathway

You can never step into the same river; for new
waters are always flowing on to you.

- Heraclitus

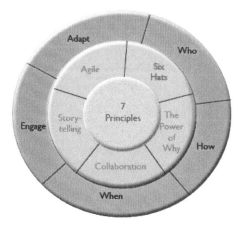

This section explores the Five Steps in the engagement pathway. Each step includes a number of practices and techniques. Each chapter ends with suggestions of the contexts when each step should be used, and how the step lives the seven principles.

CHAPTER 9

The Who Step: Knowing your stakeholders

You can forget important stakeholders, but they won't forget you.

- With apologies to Tom Gilb[1]

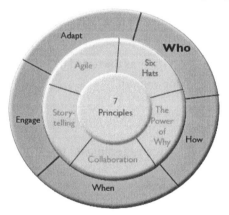

F inding out who your stakeholders really are and understanding them is a crucial early step. If anything, most managers err on the side of underestimating who qualifies as a 'stakeholder'. But no one likes to feel they have been left out. If someone feels ignored, excluded or dismissed to the sidelines by your focus, then you shouldn't be surprised if they get upset and resist what you are trying to do. Anyone who otherwise might have little interest in your work can become suspicious, albeit unnecessarily, if they find that they have not been considered or consulted.

---

1   Tom Gilb's 'Third Wave Principle' reads: "You may forget some critical factors, but they won't forget you," on page 19 of his classic *Principles of Software Engineering Management* (1988). My contention throughout this book is that certain relationships are critical factors.

Further, we must try to gain an accurate picture of stakeholders. Getting this wrong can start a stakeholder relationship in a poor way from which it is sometimes is difficult to recover. Why make your work harder? Making few, if any, assumptions about your stakeholder and finding out about them is time well spent.

Practice: Running a stakeholder workshop [Leader, Change Agent]

You almost always identify a richer set of stakeholders in a workshop with others involved in the change than you would do by making a list on your own.

Discuss with your sponsor or director who else you could invite in addition to your team members. This is an opportunity to start engaging with a few key stakeholders by inviting them as well. Feeling part of shaping the change is a strong means of building commitment to the change, as we saw in Chapter 6.

Use an independent facilitator if you can; it can be quite liberating. You can allow yourself to contribute as fully as the rest of the group. If you can't, then be prepared to lead the workshop yourself.

Technique: Rapid listing [Marketer]

One of the quickest and most robust techniques for identifying stakeholders at the start is to:

1. Gather your core team together.

2. Explain what you mean by a 'stakeholder' and why it is important the team does not miss anyone.

3. Get each individual to make a rapid personal list of everyone they can think of, giving them about three minutes to do this.

4. Pair people off and ask them to compare their lists, adding new stakeholders as they occur to them.

5. Move these pairs into groups of four and repeat the last step.

6. Finally ask the whole team to make a joint list.

Technique: Segmenting [Marketer]

Segmenting involves taking a large group and dividing them into smaller groups or segments, according to similar characteristics or perspectives, in order to tailor different approaches for each segment.

We will develop this idea further, but here it is helpful to start with some generic categories of stakeholders. We'll call these categories our segments.

Here are four segments:

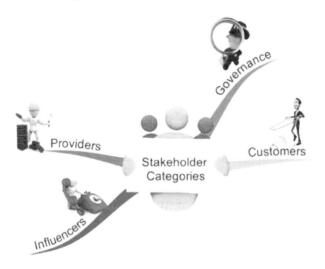

Figure 17 : Four Stakeholder Categories/Segments

Customers

These are the people who will consume or use what you deliver, either directly or indirectly, who will achieve the outcomes beyond what you deliver, and therefore they will realise the benefits from what you deliver.

'Customers' are sometimes proxy customers: people within your organisation who claim to speak on behalf of external customers. Take care with these people. Proxy customers, as with focus groups, can offer you a distorted picture of what real customers actually want, feel, and how they might react. Always try to identify the ultimate customers and, if possible, engage with them directly.

Providers

These could be key suppliers or minor suppliers, partners or commodity providers. These stakeholders are sources of the skills and resources you need. They can be both external and internal. These could be stakeholders actively involved in designing, building, testing and deploying the solution. If you are the project manager, then many of the providers might report to you, either directly or indirectly. The people who directly report to you constitute your project team.

Influencers

Influencers can affect the course of your change or even stop it, even though in some cases they might not even be aware of it. They create a sort of risk environment for the whole venture. Press and media, trade unions and professional bodies are typical influencers.

Governance

This segment includes the decision-makers and those who support them. Governance as a segment is layered. Within a project you not only need to consider the stakeholders on your project board, but maybe also others in the programme that commissioned your project, as well as the corporate portfolio management of all projects and programmes within the organisation.

There are other classifications that we will consider later, but all stakeholders can be resolved into these four. For example, government agencies could be external Governance stakeholders. At this point in the Who Step, the issue is not so much to argue which categories each falls within, so much as making sure you include all stakeholders.

Middles

Barry Oshry presents a fascinating analysis of dysfunction in most large organisations of what he calls "System Blindness". He segments the stakeholders in the system into the Tops, Middles, Bottoms, and Customers.

The Tops are in a condition of **Overload**. As the overseers of a complex system, they are continually absorbed with complex changing problems, that have been escalated upwards.

The Middles are **Crunched** in between the Tops and the Bottoms, often feeling pulled between the conflicting demands of the other two. Not only that but they feel pulled apart from each other.

The Bottoms feel **Disregarded**. They have ideas, but they have problems both with the system and the feeling that the Tops and the Middles are not fixing the problems they ought.

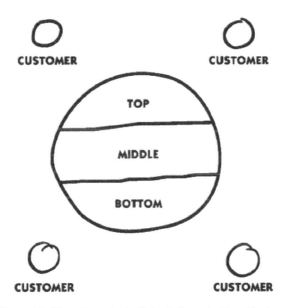

Figure 18 : The categories in Oshry's Organisational System

Customers feel **Neglect**. For them, products and services are not being shipped fast enough or with sufficient quality or at an appropriate price. They complain of inadequate responsiveness.

Oshry argues for system self-awareness by all the constituents as the route to a more robust, healthy organisation. For our purposes, it is quite likely that we see these responses and complaints from all these stakeholders.

Refer to Oshry's work for ways to create positive leadership from Middles (as well as Tops). He demonstrates the powerfully positive part middles can play in enabling successful change.

Technique: Brainstorm/Mind Map stakeholders [Change Agent]

Divide the participants into two or more groups to brainstorm 'Who are our stakeholders?' They can produce a list on flip charts or using sticky notes.

In order to get people thinking, you might like to show a generic set of categories of stakeholder, such as in Figure 16 above, in the form of a Mind Map.

To an extent, the Mind Map form gives a greater degree of freedom to continue to add branches. However, if the groups are generating lists instead make groups keep going after completing the first flip chart sheet.

Have you noticed how often groups feel they are finished simply because the first flip sheet is full? This began to happen on one workshop I facilitated. I encouraged them to keep going and it led to the list growing to identifying critical stakeholders they had not previously considered, something that became vital later.

Then get the groups to compare their lists. Invariably they differ, so you end up with a larger, richer stakeholder list, even larger, probably, when the groups all discuss together.

Another approach is to rotate the groups to validate, question, add and amend to other groups' lists.

Not all of the types of stakeholder will apply to every change initiative in your organisation. For example, you may have an internal project being executed in an environment that is of no interest to Trades Unions or Shareholders.

Understanding your stakeholders

> Einstein's wife was once asked if she understood the theory of relativity, and she replied, 'No, but I understand Einstein.'
>
> **—Selwyn Hughes**

Merely identifying your stakeholders only takes you part of the way forward. In order to engage with these stakeholders well you will need to understand them to some extent and be able to anticipate how they might react to what you are proposing and doing.

The main aspects to analyse are:

- Formal position or role towards the change

- Nature of their interests

- Level of their interest

- Attitudes towards your initiative

- Support and relationships with other stakeholders

- Level of influence and power

- Likely wins and losses from the change

- Likely readiness for change

- Likely resistance to change.

Of course, these factors are not independent of each other, as this Mind Map shows:

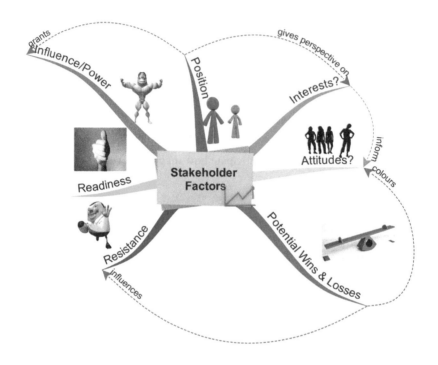

Figure 19 : The interrelationship of Different Stakeholder Factors

In using the stakeholder workshop and allied techniques, you will have already begun to take a view on these aspects with some of your stakeholders. However, the logical distinction between identifying stakeholders and analysing them is helpful. As we've already noted, scampering on without a full identification of all the stakeholders will harm you later. However, identifying and analysing stakeholders do overlap in practice. Here you focus on gaining a deeper insight into where your stakeholders are coming from, what they are like. This will serve you well when you find yourself in the thick of things, when holding difficult conversations with people.

Rapport

Perhaps one of the most fascinating studies Pink quotes is of call centre sales people. The graph below plots sales revenue on an Extroversion-Introversion axis. From the graph it is clear that it is those between the two extremes, people who are able to adjust their style, the 'Ambiverts', who are more successful in selling. The old stereotype has it that successful sales people are all extroverts. The evidence shows otherwise. Perhaps this is because the Ambiverts can better track, adjust and build a rapport with the people they are seeking to influence.

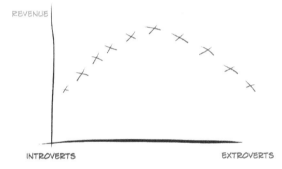

Figure 20 : Sales Revenue by Level of Extroversion

Most of the practices and techniques that analyse your stakeholders express this other-perspective[2]. Think of other-perspective as a competence or a life skill. The better you become at tuning into people, the more effective you will become in practising what follows.

---

2   This concept was introduced in the first principle.

Technique: Matching [Change Agent]

Neuro-linguistic programming, or NLP as it is more commonly known, has grown as a body of techniques from the work of Richard Bandler and John Grinder.[3] Collectively these techniques attempt to model the behaviour patterns of 'exceptional' people. One such NLP technique – Matching - might be relevant here. This is a technique where you mimic key aspects of behaviour (first body language, then voice tone and pace, and finally words). If they lean forward, so do you. If they open their hands, so do you. BUT this comes with a health warning: it can backfire seriously if the other party feels you are manipulating them with it. It should be done discreetly, subtly and strategically. It works, it seems, partly because humans trust those more like themselves.

---

3   *Frogs into Princes: Neuro Linguistic Programming.* (Real People Press, 1979).

Practice: Understanding your stakeholder interests [Politician, Change Agent]

Think about what interests each stakeholder in and around the change, or as a consequence of the change. Ask, 'Is this interest shared by other stakeholders also?'

You can capture the stakeholders and their interests on a table thus:

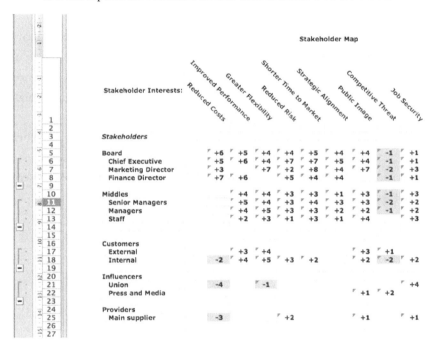

Figure 21 : Stakeholder interests mapped on a spreadsheet

The stakeholders are listed down the left-hand column and their interests are listed across the top. Often you will have a stakeholder within a stakeholder. In this example (Figure 20) there is 'the Board' but within it three directors have been separately identified, within their own variance from the group interests. Since this table is generated with a spreadsheet, stakeholders can be nested within stakeholders (e.g. an individual within a group), as shown in the extreme left grey area of this screen shot. The Finance Director as an individual, may have a different or more specific agenda than her other colleagues on the Board; so the team need to identify her separately for special analysis.

This type of map includes positive and negative attitudes as noted by the shade of the cells. Also the strength of the interest by each stakeholder is indicated by a positive or negative number. There are a number of variations of these sorts of tables or maps.

Note that people are often more comfortable with talking in broad terms about groups and bodies: the Board, the Executive Team, the HR function or the IT Group, but it is the individuals within these that we need to influence. For influential stakeholders it is essential that we identify the key individuals within them.

You can use this table as a checklist in communications planning (When step); you can check whether you are covering off everything of interest with each stakeholder. As you go through the Engage step with your stakeholders, validate your understanding and change the table entries as need be.

Practice: Analysing attitude [Politician]

A great many people think they are thinking when
they are rearranging their prejudices.

—William James

"Attitude" is a broad qualitative term, so adding some working classification is helpful. In his book Working the Shadow Side, Gerard Egan[4] suggests putting all stakeholders into the following categories:

- Your **partners** are those who support your agenda

- Your **allies** are those who will support you given encouragement

- Your **fellow travellers** are passive supporters who may be committed to the agenda but not to you personally

- The **fence sitters** are those whose allegiances are not clear

- **Loose cannons** are dangerous because they can vote against agendas in which they have no direct interest

- Your **opponents** are players who oppose your agenda but not you personally

- Your **adversaries** are players who oppose both you and your agenda

- **Bedfellows** are those who support the agenda but may not know or trust you

- The **voiceless** are stakeholders who will be affected by the agenda but have little power to promote or oppose and who lack advocates.

As you work through these categories on all the stakeholders you have listed, you will find it helps you to think more deeply about the motives and interests of each stakeholder. Also as you categorise stakeholders this way, you begin to think through different engagement strategies for each. (See the How Step below).

---

4   *Working the Shadow Side: A Guide to Positive Behind-the-Scenes Management* (Jossey-Bass, 1994).

Technique: Power mapping [Politician]

As we have recognised earlier, where real power lies is not always immediately obvious. In some organisations, some people wield influence and power disproportionate to their formal position. There may be formal authority vested in someone's role in a organisation, but often people lower down in the authority hierarchy "punch above their weight"; they are more powerful than might first appear from an organisation chart. For example, someone in a junior position has power because they are the partner of the Sales Director.

Power Maps are useful when you want to identify the key influencers among a small group. This technique is used by some sales people for identifying the key influencer in a buying decision in a target organisation.

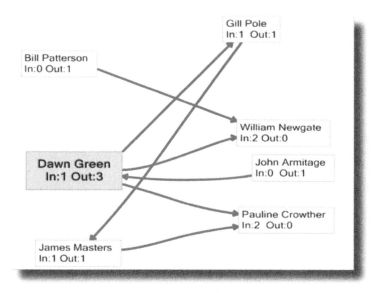

Figure 22 : An example Power Map

Here's how you use this technique:

1. Agree on, and gain, a common understanding of the context that the group of people is to be studied under, e.g. subject area, project team.

2. Summarise the context in a short sentence.

3. List all the people involved.

4. Arrange their names in a circle on a flip chart or white board. Leave plenty of space between the names for adding arrows later.

5. Look for cause/influence relationships between each of the people and connect them with arrows. If there is no influence relationship between the people, omit the arrow. If there is a relationship, the point of the arrow needs to go to the person that is most influenced. Do not draw two-headed arrows. Base your decision on the behaviours you have seen and experienced.

6. Check the diagram is complete and accurate.

7. Tally the number of ingoing and outgoing arrows for each person.

8. Redraw the diagram including the number of ingoing and outgoing arrows for each person. Highlight the person with the most outgoings as the likely key influencer in the context.

9. Initially focus on the key influencer; this is likely to be your point of maximum leverage in the context.

Caution: In common with several other similar techniques, this analysis is fairly sensitive. In the wrong hands it could be construed as manipulative. If you use this technique, have a care about where this analysis is kept and how it is used.

Technique: The persona & empathy mapping [Marketer]

The word 'Persona' is defined as "the social role or character played by an actor", from the Latin word meaning "mask". In marketing, though, it is typically used as a summary for a group of customers, but written as if it were an individual.

You create a persona for a stakeholder that represents a group, so that you can better empathise with the group's goals and needs, and shape your messages in a way that is more likely to influence them. This makes it easier for you and your team to focus on a manageable set of personas, knowing they represent the needs of many.

With this technique, you make up the persona's fictitious name. Be relevant and serious; humour usually is not appropriate.

Generally, personas are given a picture. You can use stock photography, although teams often find a more casual photo resonates with them. Avoid using a picture of someone the team knows. A good test of the photo or picture will be when someone in your team feels that the persona reminds them of someone in the group, but is not an actual photo of them.

By using the challenging question: "Would Bill do this?" - where 'Bill' is a persona (see below) - you and your team can avoid the common error of providing what people ask for rather than what they would actually use.

Engaging with groups can be constantly evaluated against the personas. If we disagree over how we engage with a group as a stakeholder, then this can often be resolved by referring back to the persona.

Caution: There is a danger that we all reinforce social stereotypes. Be careful with this, and have someone in the group who challenges excessive caricatures of the people represented.

Cooper[5] summarised the benefits of using personas:

1. They help team members share a specific, consistent understanding of various audience groups. Data about the groups can be put in a proper context and can be understood and remembered in coherent stories.

---

5   Cooper, Alan. *The Inmates are Running the Asylum*. SAMS, 1999

2. Proposed solutions can be guided by how well they meet the needs of individual personas. Features can be prioritised based on how well they address the needs of one or more personas.

3. They provide a human "face" so as to focus empathy on the persons represented by the demographics.

An example persona

The stakeholder group illustrated here is plant managers within a utility business. The persona of Bill has been created to represent a typical member of this group.

Bill is 42, and has worked in the Company since leaving school. He started as an apprentice and has worked his way to this role through being promoted internally. He has an HNC in water mechanics. He has a wife and three children, two of them pre-school. He is a member of a Trades Union and used to be Shop Steward for another plant until he was promoted to Plant Manager.

At the moment he is struggling to make ends meet as his mortgage repayments have increased. His wife is considering working evenings in a restaurant. He feels he is underpaid for the extra responsibilities of being the Plant Manager.

Empathy mapping

The empathy map is a supporting technique using a persona that has been used to some effect with a range of organisations. The map helps you devise stronger strategies for engaging with such groups.

As you can see, the upper part of the map radiates out from the image of the persona:

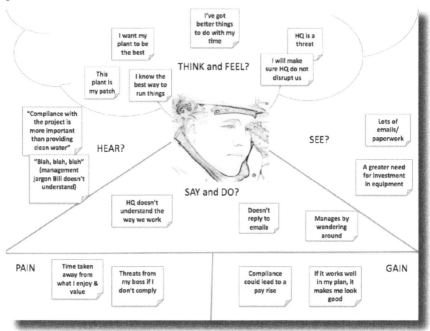

Figure 23 : An Empathy Map

1.   Radiating out of the top of the head is the question: "What does he really **think and feel**?" This is where you try to describe what is on Bill's mind. There might be matters really important to Bill that he might not disclose. This is the area to speculate about his motivations, and emotions; about what concerns him, makes him anxious; and about his dreams and aspirations.

2.   The sector to the left radiates out from one of his ears, and answers the question: "What does Bill really **hear**?" We need to look for evidence in conversations with him. What are his colleagues, his co-workers saying? What rumours are reaching his ears? Which media are likely to reach him?

3.   The sector to the right radiates out of Bill's eyes, and answers the question: "What does he **see**?" It describes what he observes in his environment. What do his surroundings look like? Who are his friends and the people who influence his opinions? What are the propositions put to him each day? What are the problems Bill has to grapple with?

4.   The lower sector is about what Bill **says and does**. It's about his words and actions. What is his attitude? What could he be telling others about your initiative? Look for potential conflicts with what Bill says and what he truly feels. This has consequences when you leave his plant. To what behaviour does he revert?

The final two sections at the bottom of the map are pain and gain:

5.   What is Bill's **pain**? What are his biggest frustrations? Have you asked him? What are the perceived obstacles standing between Bill and what he wants to achieve? Are there any risks he might fear taking? Is there additional pain that you bring to him with your change?

6.   What does Bill stand to **gain**? What does he truly want or need to achieve? How does he measure success? What ways might he use the change to achieve his own goals?

Here are some simple steps to generating a useful empathy map:

- Start by giving the group an individual persona.

- Refer to the diagram and draft this face and sectors onto a flip chart or white board.

- Build a profile with your team for the persona/stakeholder using the questions above.

Technique: Two-dimensional stakeholder maps [Politician, Change Agent]

There are many different ways people have mapped stakeholders. One of the most enduring and useful ways is by looking at each stakeholder in terms of their power/influence over your change against their actual interest in it.

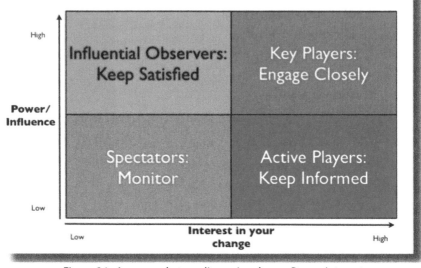

Figure 24 : An example two-dimensional map: Power-Interest

Stakeholders (groups or individuals) can then be plotted on this grid. Sometimes, the grids can be used for targeting. For example, a powerful stakeholder in 'Influential Observers' needs to move to 'Key Players'; that is to say, we need them to buy-in and be engaged more actively. It is just as important to ensure we keep certain 'Key Players' in that quadrant and not drift into disinterest.

Other common combinations of grid axes are:

- Trust v alignment/consensus

- Impact of the change on the stakeholder v influence

- Power v commitment to the change

- Energy v commitment to the change

- Change readiness v commitment to the change.

The technique can be used as part of a stakeholder workshop, when the group or its facilitator feels it can move beyond identification.

Don't obsess about the exact placement of a stakeholder on these ranges; as the British Economist John Kay[6] puts it, beware of 'bogus quantification'. In a workshop participants can agree who falls where by consensus. Often it is the insight arising out of these discussions that proves the most valuable.

> On one of my own projects, the Marketing Director of New Media was someone of High Influence, and the performance of his line of business was going to be directly affected by my project's outcome (High Interest). So he was a Key Player. I needed him on board every step of the way.
>
> This led me to seek frequent 'face time' with him, usually on a one-to-one basis. Whereas, another stakeholder on the same project was the IT Network Manager, and his influence was marginal and neither the project nor its outcome would change his working life much; most of the time I just needed to keep him informed as a matter of courtesy.

You are aiming for appropriate engagement in the later steps (the When and the Engage Steps). You should be able to engage with people differently but appropriately. For example, simply blasting everyone with the same mass email is very unlikely to achieve the results you want, and possibly will trigger some consequences you don't want.

---

6   *Obliquity: Why Goals are Best Achieved Indirectly* (Profile: 2011)

Technique: Stakeholder profiling [Change Agent]

Whilst a persona/empathy map might be a powerful tool for selected groups, it is clearly not appropriate or practicable for all your stakeholders. Some management approaches suggest documenting a profile for each stakeholder. Here are the typical contents of such a profile:

- Stakeholder **name**. Make sure it is unique and whether it is a group or an individual

- Stakeholder **interest in your change our its outcome**

- **Level of impact on the stakeholder**: High, Medium, Low

- **Level of influence or power which the Stakeholder has over your initiative and/or its outcome**: High, Medium, Low

- **Attitude towards your initiative** or project and its outcome: use a range such as A-N-A-H-M: 'Anti', 'Neutral', 'Allow it to Happen', 'Help it to Happen', 'Make it Happen'. Include the current and target **positions**

- **Ability** position: such as A-I-E-P-E, Aware', 'Informed', 'Equipped', 'Practiced', 'Exemplar Practitioner' or the DREAM scale of: 'Disengaged', 'Resistant', 'Exploring', 'Able', and 'Models'

- **Benefits** to them

- **Dis-benefits**[7] to them

- **Perceived resistance** (if any)

- **Change readiness**: how ready is the stakeholder to make the change

- (Perceived) **risks** to them

- Date **last contacted**

---

7   A "dis-benefit' is something that disadvantages a stakeholder by what you do in the project or as a consequence of the project. For example, they might be moved to a less attractive work area. A dis-benefit is not treated as a risk since it is something that will happen because of the project. So the engagement responsibility is partly to manage down dis-benefits. See the practice below of assessing potential wins and losses.

- **Changes needed from the stakeholder**

- **Satisfaction rating**: how satisfied the stakeholder perceives they are with the change

- **Next step** that could/should be taken with that stakeholder relationship.

The profile is used to track a stakeholder through your project and beyond. An internal customer relationship management (CRM) system can be used to record these profiles.

Another alternative is to chart each stakeholder profile as part of a spreadsheet that can then generate charts on any two attributes for all the stakeholders. (See 'Mapping Stakeholders by two-dimensional grids' above.)

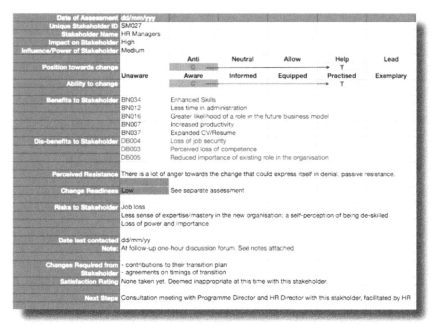

Figure 25 : An example Stakeholder Profile on a spreadsheet

This kind of record allows you and your team to see the current assessment of a stakeholder and the related issues at a glance. It begins to help you form an approach to that stakeholder, and perhaps other stakeholders, that we explore later.

Practice: Assessing potential wins and losses [Accountant, Politician]

People only listen to one radio station:
WII-FM (What's In It For Me).

—Ed Eggling

A hot topic that runs through most engagements is discussing outcomes and benefits; stakeholders will ask "What will happen?' 'What's in it for me' (WIIFM). Even if they don't ask these questions, it is usually helpful to raise these with them at the right moment.

For example, the "Gains" section in the empathy map can be used to record the benefits of the change to the persona/Stakeholder.

No stakeholder analysis is complete without thinking of such benefits for each stakeholder concerned. Frequently change creates outcomes that are perceived as negative by some: a so-called dis-benefit. For example, 'reducing headcount' might be a benefit to senior management, but is a dis-benefit to you if it means losing your job!

Using the Benefits Distribution Table[8] (Figure 25) helps you identify all the perceived benefits and dis-benefits for each stakeholder. Moreover, it gives sight of the balance between benefits and dis-benefits. This balance is a good indicator of the likely response from that stakeholder to your change.

People tend to focus on the negative more than the positive when it comes to any change imposed on them, so in the above example we can expect the business users to be fairly resistant.

---

8   Used with kind permission of Sigma UK Limited.

Key benefits and disbenefits by stakeholder	Executive Management	Business Management	Business Users	IS Function	Programme Team	Finance Function
Key Benefits						
More effective project portfolio						
Earlier recognition of ineffective projects						
More financial benefits realised						
More non-financial benefits realised						
Improved management of risk						
Reduced IS/IT costs						
Improved image of IS/IT						
Key Disbenefits						
Extra effort by business						
Slower start to programme						
IS Project Targets threatened						

Figure 26 : The benefits distribution table

If you adopt the technique of compiling stakeholder profiles in a spreadsheet (see the stakeholder profile technique above) then it is fairly easy to generate this table.

The accountant's perspective would regard this as a stakeholder profit and loss account. So the accountant would be looking for ways to move towards an "everybody is a net gainer/winner". Whilst rarely possible, this approach can help identify risks across your mix of stakeholders and make you aware of those who think they stand to lose overall.

Practice: Assessing resistance and readiness [Change Agent]

> The direct use of force is such a poor solution to any problem. It
> is generally employed only by small children and large nations.

> **—David Friedman**

These are two related concepts:

- How **resistant** is the stakeholder to change?
- How **ready** is the stakeholder to change?

They may not be resistant, but neither may they be ready. They might find themselves unable even to acknowledge the change and the losses it implies to them.

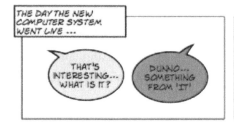 

You need to assess when your client community is ready for receiving your work and for all the change that using it will imply. Some elements of readiness are, of course, extremely difficult to measure, but they must be recognised, rather than ignored.

The following is a powerful checklist that you can use to take an informed view on resistance and readiness:

1. Do you have effective ways of **liaising** with this stakeholder and others throughout your project? It is a concern if there is no way to communicate appropriately with them, for example, if you need to meet with them and this proves difficult. How amenable are they to making themselves available?

2.   What is the **trust** level like between you and the stakeholder, the trust the stakeholder has in the wider organisation? Lack of trust is likely to stop optimal change ever happening. Do you need to set about building or restoring that trust? Are there ways you can demonstrate your trustworthiness?

3.   Has the stakeholder **understood the underlying reasons** for the change and the pressure that this creates? This is both to do with the external drivers acting upon the organisation and its response expressed partly with the change as an enabler of a better future. Does the stakeholder have a clear vision of that future?

4.   What sort of evidence are you able to find about the stakeholder's **motivation and willingness to act**?

5.   What is the **history of change** within the stakeholder's part of the organisation, its track record? In particular, recent history will colour people's view of the expected pain of the change and its viability. How much will recent history affect whether they believe the change will be carried through to success?

6.   Is there a close fit between the proposed change and the **values/ culture of the stakeholder**? Be aware that a change sometimes goes deeper than merely changing working practices.

7.   What is the individual's **own history of change**? It may be that the reactions to your change will spark associations with recent, often unwelcome experiences of change, inside or outside the workplace. If someone is going through some traumatic changes in their private lives, they may resist any threats to the stability of their working environment rather more than is otherwise reasonable.

8.   Does the stakeholder have enough capable people with resources to support this change, given its volume, the competence required of them and experience that might be needed? Is there sufficient **capacity for change** in terms of numbers, competence and experience? Are there sufficient support systems in place?

9.   What is the degree of **slack** in the stakeholder's current daily work to allow taking on board the additional work of change? Note: if there is no slack, then expect resistance, "We're too busy to think about that right now..." How could you help the stakeholder build in some slack? Back-filling? Bringing in temporary help?

10.   What are the incentives or **rewards** – and not just monetary ones - that can be offered to the stakeholder?

11.   Does the stakeholder organisation provide a capacity to **learn and adapt**?

12.   Is there clear **accountability** evidenced by the stakeholder towards implementing this change? Are they clear about consequences of resistance, overt or passive?

13.   First steps. Are these **clear** to the stakeholder? Are they **practicable**?

Exploring these questions with the leader of a group affected is likely to give you both a view on what is the most effective way to engage these people, as well as to assess when the change is likely to succeed, if at all.

Technique: The Stakeholder Radar
[Change Agent]

The segmenting discussed earlier can be mapped onto a stakeholder radar. In

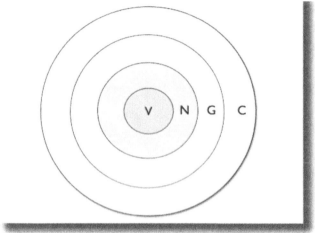

Figure 27 : The Stakeholder Radar

two dimensions, this shows not only the individual stakeholders, but also you and your team's view on the level of engagement needed with each of them. In the figure above, from the centre the different levels of engagement are labeled:

V for **v**ital to engage

N for **n**ecessary to engage

G for **g**ood to have engaged, and

C **c**ourtesy to inform.

The radar is segmented into the four domains of customers, providers, influencers and governance (Figure 28). The boundaries are porous; i.e. a stakeholder may straddle more than one domain, and cross to another domain during the life of the change.

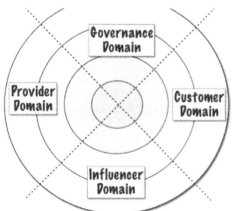

Figure 28 : Segmenting the Stakeholder Radar

Stakeholders are plotted on the radar, and the primary question becomes: How close are they to the centre? You and your team can begin to populate the Radar as follows:

In the example below, the Programme Director is right in the centre, whilst other stakeholders fan out into different domains. Note as well how the Existing Supplier is closer to the centre than the shortlisted supplier, as they are rather more engaged with the changes taking place.

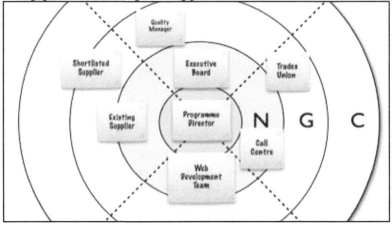

Figure 29 : Stakeholders plotted on the Radar

A short checklist for stakeholder analysis

So, what are the essential points we need to address in this Who Step? Use this short checklist:

- How much buy-in is needed from each stakeholder? Therefore how involved do they need to be in the planning?

- How good is your relationship with the key stakeholders – and does this need to improve? How will you go about this?

- Which stakeholders have enough power to cause trouble because they either don't like you or they don't like your agenda, and how will you deal with this?

- How can you get your allies to help promote the change? What will you want from your sponsor?

- How do you want to deal with the voiceless? What are your values through this change?

Living the principles in the Who Step

Seek first to understand, and then be understood: This Step is all about gaining an adequate understanding of your stakeholders. Also, by inviting key stakeholders to your workshop, you will gain an even greater understanding of them, and they of you and your agenda.

Effective change is always led: All good leaders make a study of those they seek to lead. This step is very natural to the leader. It sets you up to lead well.

Habits are the inhibitors and the goal: Analysing their attitudes, personas and empathy mapping all touch on existing cultural habits that might create resistance. Assessing the potential wins and losses, and assessing resistance and change readiness, will throw into sharp relief any current inhibiting practices among your stakeholders.

Recognise and minimise the pain of change: This Step is more relevant to living the first half of this principle, where the pain that your change might inflict on your stakeholders becomes clearer. The How Step goes on to consider how to reduce, eliminate or even avoid this pain.

High performance comes through people and action: Involving key stakeholders in your stakeholder workshops is living this principle.

Integrity is powerfully persuasive: Integrity is more easily lived out in later steps in the engagement pathway if you are prepared for the push-backs and objections your stakeholder community might express later.

Feelings trump reason, and meaning trumps authority: The geography of emotions and meaning are mapped out by using empathy mapping, assessing the benefits and dis-benefits in the wins and losses analysis. The latter also explores the meaning for each stakeholder, their "WIIFM" (what's in it for me).

When to use this Step

- Before your change initiative even begins

- When you find yourself surprised by some unexpected stakeholder reaction – positive or negative

- When you receive a call or an email from some aggrieved person you've never heard of, who asks why you haven't invited them to a meeting or consulted them about this

- At the end of every phase of your engagement as laid out in your strategy and plan.

Who Step - Summary

- The risk to avoid here is missing or forgetting people: "You can forget important stakeholders, but they won't forget you." You don't want to draw your net too narrowly in thinking about the people you need to engage. There are probably more stakeholders than you first realise, and forgetting them is dangerous

- Identifying stakeholders is better done as a group in a workshop. Consider a facilitated stakeholder analysis workshop

- Stakeholder engagement is a journey. As you start talking with people, you will identify further stakeholders and new or changed interests. You need to regularly revisit this Step

- Know your stakeholders in terms of their:

  Interests
  Influence and impact
  Attitudes and motivations
  Ability towards helping the change
  Gains (benefits) to them and losses (dis-benefits)
  Perceived resistance
  Change readiness
  Risks to them
  When last engaged
  Changes needed from them
  Their satisfaction rating with the change
  The next step with them

- Stakeholders that are groups may be analysed to some effect with the use of personas and empathy maps

- Consider profiling each stakeholder, particularly the ones you identify as key

- Against the benefits and dis-benefits that will be realised from your change, consider how each stakeholder wins and loses. Most will have a mix, so their perceived net loss is important

- For some groups, consider drawing a power map so that you can identify the key influencers in the group

- Consider using Egan's types to classify different groups of stakeholder

- Conduct a change readiness assessment on some or all of your stakeholders

- Beware of middle managers - your least natural allies in changing for the better.

Who Practices

- Running a stakeholder workshop
- Understanding your stakeholder interests
- Analysing attitude
- Assessing' potential wins and losses
- Assessing resistance and readiness.

Who Techniques

- Rapid listing
- Segmenting
- Brainstorm/Mind Map stakeholders
- Matching
- Power mapping
- Personas

- Empathy mapping

- Two-dimensional stakeholder maps

- Stakeholder profiling

- Stakeholder radar.

CHAPTER 10

·The How Step: Shaping your engagement

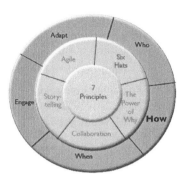

Think twice before you speak, because your words and influence will plant the seed of either success or failure in the mind of another.

—Napoleon Hill

In the Who Step you considered the profile of each stakeholder, those characteristics that might help you choose how to influence them. As you move to the How Step - shaping your strategy of engagement - you will build on this with certain approaches. For example, if you have a good grasp of the influence of each stakeholder, you will have a better understanding of where the power lies with all involved in and around your change. This will help you prioritise your efforts. Also, you need to outline the broad sequence of engagement through your change as a story.

Reasons for an engagement strategy

Before you begin to plan your communications and conversations, you will need to decide on your rules of engagement, or strategy. There are multiple reasons why you should consider this:

1. It quickly becomes obvious to you that certain stakeholders require a different treatment; for example, someone else in your team may be better positioned to engage them, or a stakeholder might be more receptive if approached in a different way.

2. Maybe a particular individual or group requires engaging at a different tempo or frequency.

3. Your whole change may need to shift its strategy part way through its life. Unless you give attention to shaping Strategy, to defining it, you may not be aware that it is not working or that it is, in fact, changing.

4. If different members of your team are engaging with different stakeholders, you need to coordinate this so that you all stick to predictable behaviours and agreed messages, as well as keeping each other informed as relationships progress. Otherwise it gets unnecessarily complicated. You risk looking incompetent if it appears to a stakeholder that you were unaware that another team member had already discussed a matter with them.

5. Having a conscious strategy helps you decide what you should and should not do. It helps you say "No" to the many worthy but distracting activities to which you might otherwise be tempted to commit yourself. A conscious strategy can save you from exhausting yourself; instead it helps you keep focused.

Change management models

Change management models are extremely helpful in shaping our overall strategy. There are a number of different models of how you might engage people and groups through change. For example, we considered one of the simpler, and most enduring, models from Kurt Lewin[1] in the second principle: Habits are the Inhibitors and the goal of change.

Over the last fifty years, quite a few other models have emerged. Here is a Mind Map of some of the models we consider in our Change Management training:

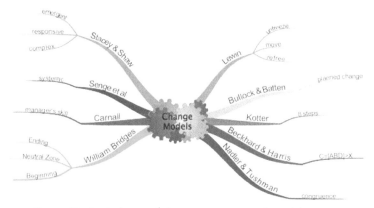

Figure 30 : A mind map of change management models

These models differ in a number of ways. So which model is the best?

All these models have survived because each of them has some merit; they each have something to offer us. Even apparently contradictory models might work in leading the same group through a change.

How can this be? Well, consider each of these models like a different golf club. A putter is designed for the green, but not much use in a bunker; a driver is definitely a choice when teeing off, but not necessarily best when you are in the rough … and so on. So a golfer plays better when she has more

---

1   Lewin, op. cit.

clubs in her bag and she knows how to use them. You could get around the
course with just a putter, but why would you want to? So it is with change
models. Change leaders find that they get better results if they employ more
than one model.

So consider developing your strategy with two or more
models. Cameron and Green[2] have written a good introductory
treatment to a number of these. Here we will consider some others,
including the Transition Planning and the Innovation Adoption
Curve.

As you get more practiced in this area you will find you
become familiar with more of these models[3]. That can only
improve your ability as a change leader.

Practice: Prioritising by innovation adoption [Marketer]

Marketers have used an approach to product promotion based upon Everett
Rogers'[4] fascinating historical study of how innovations took hold in societies.
Rogers came up with the Innovation Curve that categorises groups across a
normal distribution curve (the so-called 'bell curve') of adoption (Figure 31).

He was able to show that the first 2½% – the 'Innovators' - are not
particularly influential and are not good predictors as to whether an innovation
will ultimately be adopted or not. The Innovators are sometimes called the
'geeks': people who just love the new and will be the first to adopt anything
indiscriminately. Rogers' conclusion was that we should not give them too much
attention. They are not necessarily indicative of whether an innovation will 'take'.

It is the next 13½% - the 'Early Adopters' - who are most critical in all this.
They are also known as the **Opinion Leaders**. They are discriminating, forward-
thinking progressives. If all of the Early Adopters go with a new practice or
innovation, then the Early Majority (next 34%) will be persuaded to follow suit.
In turn, the Late Majority will follow – because "everybody" appears to be doing
it.

---

2   *Making Sense of Change Management*, 3rd Edition, (Kogan Page: 2012).
3   Consider training courses such as the 'Change Management Practitioner'.
4   *Diffusion of Innovations* (Simon & Schuster, 2004).

Finally, reluctantly, the Laggards will follow. In some versions of Rogers'

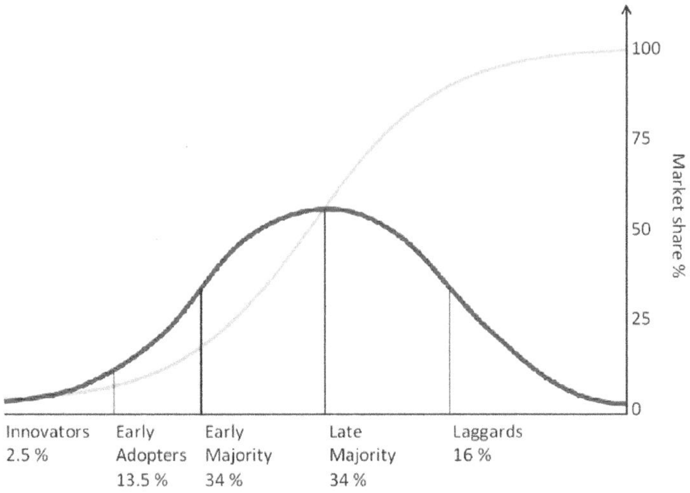

Figure 31 : The Innovation Adoption Curve

model there is a final 2½% who will never come on board with the new. So the message is: don't knock yourself out trying to persuade the last 2½% to join; leave them be or let them leave.

Marketing professionals have adopted this model with enthusiasm because it helps them track a new product's penetration into a market.

This model is relevant if you have a large population of stakeholders who all seem to have more or less the same power. Identify and target the Early Adopters and seek to recruit some of these opinion leaders to the role of Champion. For example, you could include some of these people in your stakeholder workshops, as well as asking them to take on key communication events.

Also target and track the Early Majority, not allowing yourself or your team to be distracted by the apparent apathy or resistance of the Late Majority.

Using this model in this way you can give an overall shape to your strategy, build momentum, and reassure key stakeholders that buy-in is proceeding in a predictable manner.

One way of identifying Early Adopters is to search for groups and individuals that have high levels of change readiness. These could be candidates for early prototypes. Jerry Sternin's[5] experience in post-war Vietnam, seeking to address structural child malnutrition, gained huge success by looking for 'positive deviants', or as the Heath brothers called them, 'Bright Spots'.[6] These bright spots - mothers who had positive nutritional and parenting behaviours - became champions or models for other mothers, and so began to win over the majority. This effected a cultural change across the nation in how to nourish young children.

Technique: Customer segmentation [Marketer]

The categorisation of all stakeholders into four groups introduced in the Who Step and used with the Stakeholder Radar is fine to start with, but is usually too crude to continue. Marketing has developed various approaches to segmentation, but customer segmentation holds the most promise for our purposes[7].

Customer segmentation is the practice of dividing a customer base into groups of individuals that are similar in specific ways relevant to marketing, such as age, gender, interests, spending habits and so on.

Customer groups represent different segments if:

- They have distinctly different needs, or a different offer

- They are reached through different distribution channels

- They require different types of relationships

- They are willing to pay for different aspects of the offer.

Customer segmentation procedures include: deciding what data will be collected and how it will be gathered; collecting data and integrating data from various sources; developing methods of data analysis for segmentation; establishing effective communication among relevant business units (such as marketing and customer service) about the segmentation; and implementing applications to deal effectively with the data and respond to the information it provides.

---

5   Pascale, Richard, Sternin, Jerry, Sternin, Monique, *The Power of Positive Deviance: How Unlikely Innovators Solve the World's Toughest Problems* (Harvard Business School Press: 2010).
6   *Switch* (2011) op cit.
7   See Osterwalder and Pigneur for a very good treatment of this.

So, with stakeholder segmentation, the key is what pattern emerges from the Who Step as your most useful target segments.

You will find customer segmentation particularly useful if your project rolls out to a broad mass of customers, either internal, external or both.

> In a large global roll-out of an SAP system, potential users were polled about their hopes and fears (attitude as well as their perceived wins and losses). From this analysis emerged country office segments, which suggested the early candidates for roll-out of the new system: UK and Germany followed closely by France and Spain.
>
> Another programme considered the segments in terms of the leap from their existing legacy systems. Some sites were more advanced, others not so. The latter group came with an existing churn of "down time" and high maintenance costs. This segment was prioritised for the new platform since the "pain" of existing systems was higher in this case.

Note: this is one of several illustrations where stakeholder engagement informs other parts of a project's management, such as the project approach and the implementation strategy.

Technique: Crafting value propositions [Marketer]

Once marketers have established their customer segments, using techniques like the persona and empathy maps, they develop a 'value proposition' they want to offer that segment of potential customers. Osterwalder and Pigneur[8] list a number of types of value proposition:

- **Newness**. Newness is particularly popular, by definition, among the Innovators who love the latest (see Roger's model above)

- **Performance**

- **Customisation**, tailored to the specific needs of individuals.

- **"Getting the job done"**

- **Design**

- **Brand/status**. What is the caché or positive regard owning the product will give to the individual in the eyes of others?

- **Price**, offering similar value at a lower price

- **Cost reduction**

- **Risk reduction**

- **Accessibility**

- **Convenience/usability.**

Notice how all these look very similar to descriptions of benefits. They should all lead to benefit propositions to the target stakeholders, answering their "WIIFM"[9].

---

8   Op cit.
9   See the "Assess wins and losses" Practice in the Who Step.

Technique: Assembling a bank of pitches [Marketer]

"Yes we can."

—Barack Obama

People may ask you at any time to explain the meaning, purpose and nature of your change and its outcomes. A bank of prepared pitches that you have rehearsed with your team can be a powerful aid in such moments. Moreover, these pitches help everyone in the engagement "stay on message" and instill a sense of confidence in your stakeholders.

> The purpose is to offer something so compelling that it begins a conversation, brings the other person in as a participant, and eventually arrives at an outcome that appeals to both of you.[10]

A bank of pitches contains persuasive words or phrases that are all variants on your proposition to stakeholders. This is similar in concept to the 'pitch book' used in investment banking. The pitch book consists of a careful arrangement and analysis of the investment considerations for a potential or current client.

Below are various styles of pitches you could include in your bank. They all share one feature in common: they each apply certain constraints to the form or wording. However, it is these constraints, as Patricia Stokes has written about elsewhere[11], that can actually serve to spur you and your team's creativity.

The user story

The user story has the power to empathise with certain stakeholders and, as we have seen[12], to connect the proposition with an explicit beneficial outcome. For example:

> As a call centre manager, I want the system to compare current response rates with past weeks, so that I can take early corrective action and adjust resource levels on shift.

---

10   *To Sell is Human*, op.cit. p.158.
11   *Creativity from Constraints: The Psychology of Breakthrough* (Springer Publishing, 2005).
12   See the Agile Chapter.

Pecha Kucha

Pecha Kucha, or PechaKucha, is an emergent form of presentation that has gained an enthusiastic following since its inception in about 2003. This is partly, I think, as a reaction to the tedious 'Death by PowerPoint' experiences we have all endured in meetings and at conferences. Its name derives from the Japanese for 'chit chat'. A Pecha Kucha presentation is 20 slides shown for exactly 20 seconds each, making six minutes 40 seconds for the total presentation. There are Pecha Kucha nights that include 8 to 14 presentations, allowing young design professionals (usually) to share their work and to get a high-energy peer group reaction.

The discipline of the Pecha Kucha is a powerful one and there are tools to shape such presentations[13].

A project could develop one or more such Pecha Kucha decks and present or publish these to their stakeholders as another valuable part of their bank of pitches.

Dan Pink[14] offers several others:

The one-word pitch

"I have only one word to say to you, Benjamin."

"Yes?"

"Plastics."

From the screenplay of 'The Graduate' [15]

This reduces the essence of the pitch to only one word, quite an extreme but nevertheless clarifying discipline. For example, in an office move to one single location from multiple satellite locations, the pitch was reduced to one word: "Gathered."

The twitter pitch

When Twitter first came on the scene, at first many of us didn't get it, me included: "Reducing a public message to the size of a text message? Really?" Yet Twitter has taken off in an astonishing way.

---

13   For example, the 'Haiku' iPad app is one I use and recommend.
14   *To Sell is Human*, op cit.
15   Embassy Pictures, 1967

Many great orators have used a similar discipline to great effect, well before Twitter came on the scene. Consider JFK's famous vision in the 1960's:

> We will put a man on the moon and return him safely before this decade is out. (77 characters.)

Here's another example:

> We will build a world-class golfing facility to host the Ryder Cup in Wales by 2010. (88 characters)
> —Sir Terry Matthews, Celtic Manor Golf Club.

This can become a powerful team exercise where the team works together within the constraint of 140 characters to craft the compelling pitch.

The question pitch

"How's that working out for you?"

—Tyler Durden, Fight Club[16]

Project managers are solution providers by profession, so it is perhaps understandable that we all too often fall into the trap of beginning with solutions for people. Dan Pink observes, "By making people work just a little harder, question pitches prompt people to come up with their own reasons for agreeing (or not)."[17]

A discomfiting question might be the best place to start:

> *If you were given $1m, what would you change around here?*

Or consider Ronald Reagan's bid for the US presidency:

> *Are you better off now than you were four years ago?*

---

16   Twentieth Century Fox Film Corporation, 1999
17   Ibid. page 163.

The Pixar Pitch

Getting a movie concept across to sceptical studio executives must be one of the hardest selling jobs around. Pixar have distilled this to a fine art with the following structure of six sequential sentences:

Once upon a time [fill in blank]

Every day [fill in blank]

One day [fill in blank]

Because of that [fill in blank]

Because of that [fill in blank]

Until finally [fill in blank]

So one programme example might be:

"Once upon a time, we used paper-based medical records. Every day these worked well, when we were all in the same building and everyone knew how to use them. One day, we became part of a larger medical community, spread across lots of hospitals and surgeries. Because of that, some of these records got lost, or damaged in transit, or even forgotten about in the glove compartments of clinicians' cars. Because of that, patients would arrive at clinics and their records would not be there. Because of that, they had to be sent away for another appointment and they got more sick, and sometimes died. Everyone was frustrated, angry and fearful. Until finally, the records were put onto an electronic system that approved people could access securely and safely, wherever they were. Patients got treated more promptly, less time was wasted, and (nearly) all lived happily ever after."

Notice that this story may seem somewhat patronising at first, but I suggest it is powerful; it connects with people. Further, it is easily remembered and repeated.

Exercise:

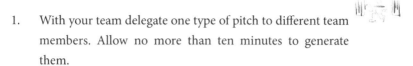

1. With your team delegate one type of pitch to different team members. Allow no more than ten minutes to generate them.

2. Place them together on a wall as a gallery and look for inconsistencies in the message.

3. Reallocate the messages to different team members and repeat 1 and 2.

4. Continue if necessary for a third round until all pitches begin to reinforce each other.

5. Discuss in what context each could be used to best effect. (Keep this step till last.)

Practice: Tracking emotional states [Change Agent]

Elizabeth Kubler-Ross[18] led a classic study into the emotional states patients went through when they were told that they were going to die. Her research showed how remarkably predictable this sequence was and that the ultimate emotional state – if the person lived long enough to experience it, that is – was often very positive indeed. She also showed that people needed time to navigate through these states: they couldn't be hurried. They needed time to 'come to terms with the situation'.

The next insight people had was that Kubler-Ross's model seems to work itself out in other less extreme situations, where someone is told other kinds of non-negotiable bad news. For example, someone is told that the job they have held for several years is going to be made redundant. Again, people begin to go through these same stages, sometimes quickly, sometimes slowly, but they all tend to follow the same sequence.

---

18   *On Death and Dying*, (MacMillan, 1969).

An adaptation and a development of her 5-step model can be shown as a graph thus:

This shows the various stages in this emotional journey:

Shock & Denial

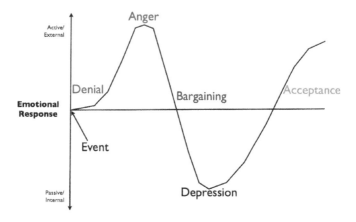

Figure 32 : Kubler-Ross - Five stages of grief

This is characterised by a sense of disbelief and non-acceptance of the change, and maybe 'proving' to oneself that it isn't happening and hoping that it will go away.

Anger

Here people experience anger and frustration, but really in an unaware sort of way, i.e. taking no responsibility for their emotions.

Bargaining & Depression

Bargaining test the news to see if it really is certain, such as, "Are you *sure* it's my name on the list. There must be a mistake." People then attempt to avoid the inevitable, hitting the lows and responding (or being unresponsive) with apathy or sadness.

Acceptance & Experimentation

Here the reality of the situation is accepted. Having been very inward looking with acceptance, the idea arrives that perhaps there are other things 'out there'. Perhaps some of these changes might be worth at least thinking about. "Perhaps I might just ask to see the job description of that new job."

As people enter this new world that has changed there may be the discovery that things aren't as bad as they imagined, perhaps the company was telling the truth when it said there would be new opportunities and a better way of working.

You can expect to find people navigating all these emotional states in contexts where they are faced with a non-negotiable change they don't initially welcome. The point is it is natural for people to go through these states.

Note that part of the graph below the horizontal line, is internally focused - the individual is absorbed with the emotions they are themselves going through, and the half above the line is externally focused, noticing what is happening externally.

Sometimes you may have gone down the curve and up the other side only to be pushed back again by some event associated with the change. It is quite possible for people to loop back. If change is badly led, that can often happen. Remember that one of our principles is to 'Minimise the pain of change'. Being careless about leading people through change, allowing them to go through the same chaos and confusion again and again is perhaps equivalent to taking a sticking plaster only part-way off the skin, losing one's nerve, sticking it back, only to find you have to revisit this unpleasantness at a later moment.

Often managers and leaders will have gone through the curve and be going up the other side. They can't understand why everyone else isn't as optimistic as they are, the reason being that other people are still going down! When on the left hand side (and internally focused) it is difficult to hear any communication from those on the right hand side. This is a known problem that medical consultants have to deal with when advising patients on the best course of treatment: shock often means that the patient simply cannot take it all in at that appointment.

Now, overlaying this curve you can see four broad attitudinal states in relation to engagement:

- Denial

- Resistant

- Exploring

- Champion.

Where there is a non-negotiable change - where people have to deal with it as there is no alternative - then you can map individual stakeholders on their emotional journey in a grid thus:

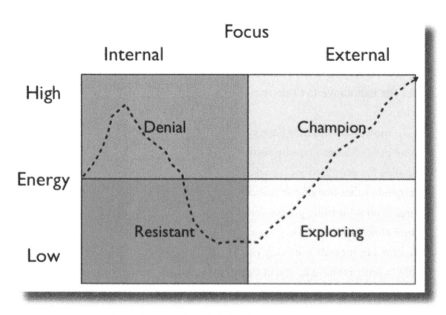

Figure 33 : Tracking stakeholder emotional states

One of our clients used this approach in centralising its geographically dispersed workforce of around 2,000 office workers into one central building. In terms of personal impact on each of these people, this was sometimes traumatic: moving home and schools, lengthening commute, etc. It was clear from the evidence that despite communications well in advance many had ignored this and were in the denial zone. As the day approached, resistance surfaced and people realised this was a real threat.

Moving people to 'exploring' was helped by personal stories and research from people who had already moved to the new location and found out about housing, schooling, and other local services first hand. Some had found real added personal benefit from improved lifestyle and this was also communicated.

The move was considered by this client to have been a success. About 200 people did not move; they either resigned, or took voluntary redundancy or earlier retirement. It was recognised that in a change on this scale you will never bring around everybody to your change[19] and it is foolish to think for a moment you can.

---

19   See the discussion about the 'Laggards' in Rogers' Innovation Model above.

Practice: Leading with the Bridges transitions model [Change Agent, Leader]

William Bridges[20] maintains that whilst we deal with the external changes, the really important matter we need to monitor and cater for is the internal transition within the people we seek to lead.

His model is similar to others in that it is in three stages:

Figure 34 : Bridges Transition Model

Bridges noticed that whenever people are asked to change, their first internal reaction is to consider what they are losing. This is the source of much initial resistance. The first stage, he says, is that for the stakeholder the beginning is actually an **ending**. They feel a sense of loss of the old. We should identify who is losing what, accept the reality and importance of subjective losses, not be surprised at "overreaction", but acknowledge the losses openly and sympathetically, accepting the signs of grieving, seeking to compensate for the losses. Be very clear on what is over and what isn't.

Organisations with clear and real values are at an advantage here. These values become the non-negotiables of change. In these disturbing moments, people look for that which is not changing. Then as leaders it is important that we mark the endings, treating the past with respect.

Then, once they have transitioned to getting used to losing the old, there is a period of disorientation, the **Neutral Zone**. Whilst this is an uncomfortable zone to travel through, it is, he points out, a time of great potential creativity. Familiar constraints may be gone. It is an opportunity to come up with new ideas, new ways of working, as well as a time when everything feels chaotic. Bridges advises leaders to attend closely to what people are saying in the neutral zone, and deal with their complaints quickly. Sometimes providing temporary systems is appropriate in the Neutral Zone. It is a time to strengthen supportive connections within the group.

20   *Managing Transitions: Making the most of change*, (Addison-Wesley, 1991).

Finally people will transition to the '**Beginning**' and be fully prepared internally to address the new. Bridges says beginnings are strange times, where we want them and fear them at the same time. You need to explain the purpose behind the outcome you seek, paint a picture of it, provide them with a clear plan, and give each person a part to play. This has to be backed up with some very serious work to embed new practices until they become routine. There is a danger here of declaring "We've arrived" too soon. Quick successes are important, as are symbols of the new identity and celebrating the success.

Practice: Monitoring and providing slack [Change Agent]

Ruthlessly eliminate busyness from your life.

—Dallas Willard

There is a myth about free time and busyness. As a manager, you may be a victim of it. The myth is that all free time is waste; therefore all free time should be identified and used up until there is none.

Figure 35 : The relationship between busyness and task focus

I've noticed that there is something about busyness that drives me to a more 'stuff'-centric focus. Excessive busyness usually becomes the enemy of that which is truly important. For our purposes, what is of paramount importance towards realising the benefits of change is leaning into relationships, and giving them more time and respect as the key for successful outcomes.

Our research into high performers revealed something further that was quite unusual. Among this sub-population there was a strong tendency for them to reserve or hold back time in every working week. This time became their *personal margin*, their buffer against the unexpected. So an unexpected demand was made of them, and their response was to draw the necessary time from this buffer.

What about the rest? Well, we found these respondents tended to schedule themselves fully, to have no reserve, so when the unexpected came along their options were:

- Work longer and later

- Work into the weekends

- Let the less important stuff fall off the end, perhaps never to be done, ever.

I suspect that there is a causal relationship between the discipline of maintaining personal margins and higher performance.

In his book, *Slack*, Tom de Marco[21] explains how this can work at an organisational level also. He uses the illustration of a tile puzzle.

What if we saw that final "space" and decided it was "waste" and so filled it with another tile? The result would simply be that we had removed all agility from the system and 'locked' it in its current state. The system now permits no change, and therefore no development and growth. It is, in effect, organisational arthritis.

So the implications are clear: we need to be careful about fully allocating some resources, because we need the system to flex, to change. This is true for you and me as individuals. It's true for the people you expect something additional from; to do something in addition to their routine work in order to achieve your change.

For example, suppose you have a customer who is a charity and your brief is to deliver an enhanced donor database with an improved set of screens. The screens may be 'improved' but will require people

---

21   *Slack: Getting Past Burnout, Busywork, and the Myth of Total Efficiency* (Dorset House, 2001).

operating the system to learn a new way of navigating them. The operators are understaffed and fully stretched. They express their stress to you, with the clear message, "Don't bother us!" They will try to fend you off. It's their coping strategy.

Your new system will improve things for them, but not until they get worse. Usually, when people have to adapt to a new way of working, develop new skills, there is a drop in their performance, the performance dip[22].

Sometimes we can misinterpret the resistance by a stakeholder as just plain awkwardness. It is often their coping mechanism, since they have no slack.

Practice: Monitoring energy and planning recovery [Leader]

One of the aspects of leadership not often discussed is this: good leaders read the energy levels around them. They are aware of changes in the "energy climate". This affects people's ability to engage, the change readiness of a stakeholder.

So consider this: are signs of low energy or low productivity in those around you always a sign of laziness?

Not always.

Stress-recovery cycles

The Human Performance Institute (HPI), a Florida-based organisation, has for years been helping top-flight athletes achieve higher performance. Their claim is that they can improve the performance of such a client by as much as 20%. How can they measure this? Well, in the upper echelons of most sports this is actually very simple: the number of tournaments each client wins each year.

What is particularly intriguing about HPI is that they achieve this almost exclusively without working on the technical skills of their clients. For example, with the golfer Mark O'Meara HPI improved his performance without reference to his swing or his putting technique. So what did they work on? HPI's framework worked on:

- Physical exercise, diet and sleep patterns
- Mental techniques of focus, concentration and visualisation

---

22   See the transition planning model later in this Chapter.

- Emotional aspects, such as self-management of "self-talk" and auto-suggestion

- Spiritual mediation techniques such as prayer and contemplation.

HPI notes that every natural system has a stress-recovery cycle. The system could be the cardiovascular system, or a particular muscle group. The length of a system cycle could vary (for example, the heart beats multiple times a minute, whilst the brain generally has a daily sleep recovery cycle), but they all share the same stress-recovery cycle. By managed exercise the stress in the cycle is slightly increased and the recovery becomes more rapid.

As a result, because of this managed cycle at several levels, HPI clients began to outperform their opponents. For example, the tennis player, Monica Seles, would find herself in the third and final set of a match against an opponent of an equivalent technical ability, but she would win because she had an edge over her opponent: she could return her heart to resting rate between serves.

HPI went to work with other groups, such as American football teams and the FBI Hostage Unit. However, when they began to coach business people they encountered a structural problem: they found many such clients didn't have work patterns of stress-recovery, but rather were 'always on', chronically stressed. As Dr Jack Groppel of HPI says, "The only time in the natural world you find a biological system in chronic stress, flat-lining, is when it is dead!"

Now this is a serious hidden issue in many work cultures. I've seen it; I consult to some of them. There is chronic stress as well as chronic exhaustion. The more self-aware people have their own strategies for gaining 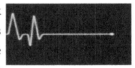 recovery: holidays, taking time off in the guise of sick leave. Sometimes, the biological systems take over for them and they naturally fall sick. But one thing is obvious: such organisations are not healthy.

Chronic busyness becomes a culture. So if we are seeking to engage individuals or groups in such cultures it gets tough.

Are they lazy or are they exhausted?

Good engagement in these cases is to become consciously counter-cultural. This means insisting that some of these people will need to get more help, to back-fill some jobs so they have the time to give to achieving the outcome they want.

It may mean insisting on 'recovery cycles' for stakeholders and being prepared to defend these on their behalf. This is one of the practices that express the principle of recognising and minimising the pain of change.

Technique: Force field analysis [Change Agent]

Lewin stresses that before change can begin, the part of the organisation that needs to change must first be 'unfrozen' from the old habits, the old status quo. Then it is fluid enough to be moved to the new. He describes how change has its own driving forces, but there always seem to be resisting forces keeping an organisation where it is. He developed the notion of force field analysis, and how leaders should seek ways of weakening the resisting forces more than seeking to increase the driving forces.

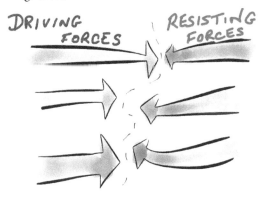

Figure 36 : Force field analysis

Exercise: Brainstorm with your team the driving forces and resisting forces on two separate lists.

Get everyone to vote on the strength of each force, say on a scale of 1-5.

Draw the driving and resisting forces on a chart with the driving forces as arrows pushing from the left, and the resisting forces pushing from the right. Draw the length of the arrows according to their strength: the larger the strength of that force, the longer the arrow.

Now challenge the workshop to consider ways of reducing or weakening the resisting forces.

The force field diagram then becomes very illuminating. Consider that what you have drawn represents 'stalemate'; nothing will change, unless the resisting forces are weakened, and unless the driving forces exceed the resisting forces.

Technique: The individual's force field [Change Agent]

Edgar Schein[23], author of process consulting, has posed a version of force field analysis that he has observed at work on individuals who face the prospect of changing their working practices. This too gives us valuable insights into how to make it easier for people to move to the new ways of working.

Figure 37 : Schein's force field analysis

Schein says that the forces at work to move an individual to new behaviours and practices create a set of **survival anxiety** forces. These constitute the risks in the individual's mind that they will be left behind, or become irrelevant in the future. It can prompt in them an eagerness to get on top of new practices being proposed and generate a desire in them to learn the skills that will ensure their survival.

---

23   *Organizational Culture and Leadership*, (Jossey-Bass, 1985).

Opposed to that are all the concerns that suggest to that person that they will never be able to master the new skills: **learning anxiety**.

If we are to succeed in leading people into new practices, then (1) their survival anxiety must be greater than their learning anxiety. That is not to say that we should increase the survival anxiety, but rather (2) seek ways to reduce or eliminate their learning anxiety, thus allowing the force field naturally to move people to new ways of working.

With this technique:

1. Brainstorm with your team the survival and learning anxieties. Be aware that your engagement with the target stakeholder may excite both sets of anxieties in them.

2. Map these out as with the force field analysis above.

3. Consider ways of weakening the learning anxiety. For example, training, coaching, help desks, FAQ sheets, job aids are good. For individuals who are particularly concerned about losing face with their peers or their superiors, consider providing e-learning or private coaching.

Technique: Transition planning
[Leader, Change Agent]

As with Lewin's model, several change models have a three-step process. With the transition planning model it is:

1. **Unfreeze**: dealing with inertia and the need to move.

2. **Transition**: moving, starting to get used to using the new thing.

3. **Refreeze**: embedding the change until it becomes the "new normal".

For example, this approach is used with the transition model in Figure 38 below.

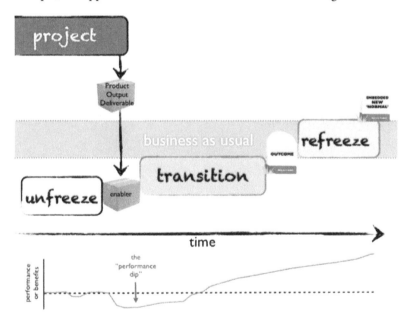

Figure 38 : The transition model

I prefer to draw this diagram for my clients, telling its story[24] as I go along. I start the story at the top of the diagram:

---

24   See video on Transition Planning:
      http://www.youtube.com/watch?v=VDd6qmTCPrY.

A project is about to come to an end. It is ready to deliver its contribution ('output'), which is a new customer relationship management system (CRM) to an operational business unit, as part of a wider programme. When it has delivered its output to requirements, the project's job will be largely done. So the business unit manager - we'll call her Lucy - has been given charge to exploit what the project hands over to her. She has been involved to a degree in the project by submitting her requirements and reviewing work, as it's been completed.

Now Lucy is expected to show an increase in a certain benefit. Let's call this benefit "an increased proportion of satisfied customers". So, in order to show the difference, Lucy measures this before the system is commissioned, during the "Unfreeze" process.

When the project delivers, the 'output' is just the beginning of the change for the business unit. From an operations perspective, it might better be called an "enabler", because it will merely enable the possibility of increasing the number of satisfied customers – the benefit she owns - to increase.

As well as measuring the 'before' state of the benefit, Lucy also calls her team together and tells them of the change that is coming. She warns them that their performance is likely to get worse rather than get better to start with, but that's OK. She tells them why they have to go through this unwelcome change. She tells them about the training and support they will be given.

Most of her team would rather this didn't happen, but after a while all concede that it has been thought through, and they trust Lucy enough to go with it for now. Some still have strong reservations, particularly about the timing. Lucy explains that the timing is the "least worst" of the alternatives the programme offered her; she made sure that the timing of when they went over to this new system was the best she could get. She stresses that keeping operations going is still her priority, but for the next few weeks, things will be complicated as they try to continue doing that and learn to use the new CRM system the project is delivering at the same time. She will be able to back-fill some work by bringing in temporary staff, but she admits this will not be a total solution.

What Lucy has been doing is the necessary leadership work within 'Unfreeze'.

Then the day arrives when the new system is commissioned. And for Lucy and her team it is tough. Performance does dip quite dramatically. Although a number of her team have had training, as is often the case, the training does not prepare them for all the specific needs at that moment. Several of her team want to abandon the conversion to the CRM and revert to the old system until it is sorted out. But she persists, and uses special temporary support from a help desk to work through their problems. The first week feels brutal but it does gradually get easier. Some of her team have begun to appreciate some of the benefits to them, and find that aspects are easier to use than the old system. Lucy notes these and feeds them back in the daily briefing meetings.

Now she finds that everyone is using the new CRM. Some are still grumbling, and performance is still poor. But she has an outcome: everyone has adopted the new system. She continues to work on coaching people up to fluent use of the new system and, as she measures the number of satisfied customers, she finds the number has begun to increase. It does not feel like this is what is happening to some in her team, but she makes sure that everyone knows that this is the reality, thanks the team, and encourages them to keep on. They had kept the old CRM going as a safety net; Lucy now instructs IT to decommission it. This is all part of 'Refreeze'. She is moving her team to the point where the new CRM is no longer regarded as 'new' but just the normal tool they use in sharing customer information.

A few weeks further on, the change has now stuck. It is now part of the new normal. And by tracking the benefits she is able to prove that all this pain was worth it. However, Lucy and her team knew that 'Refreeze' would only be temporary. Theirs is a fast-moving organisation, with continuous improvement and iterative agile practices. There would be more change soon, but now it was likely to be more sustainable.

Can you see how Lucy could work with her project manager (and the wider programme team) on a strategy for engagement? Also notice how she worked to weaken the learning anxieties within her team. If this implementation were to be replicated in the same programme in the same organisation - say with a roll-out to different departments or sites or countries - then the early experiences would be extremely useful in improving the game plan for later transitions[25].

---

25   See Appendix A.

Practice: Targeting positions [Change Agent]

In terms of co-operation, you can target the level of engagement where you intend a stakeholder to move along a spectrum from 'Anti', 'No Commitment', 'Allow it to happen', 'Help it Happen' through to 'Make it happen'.

Use the chart illustrated below by Benjamin and Levinson[26].

Stakeholder Group	Perceived Benefits (Disbenefits)	Changes Needed	Perceived Resistance	Commitment (Current and Required)					
				Anti	None	Allow it to Happen	Help it to Happen	Make it Happen	
Customers	Configuration tailored exactly to needs - no testing/reject	None	None						
Sales and Marketing Managers	Improved customer service and product quality image	New incentives to get the sales reps to use with the Customers	Reluctance to change the reps reward systems			C —	Action Required?	→ R	
Sales Reps	(Extra work in preparing requirements and quotes)	To use system and improve quality/accuracy of quotes	No time to use / learn system. Loss of autonomy.	C —		Action Required?		→ R	
Manufacturing /Logistics	Removes need for configuration checking. Less returns/queries.	Stop current checks to put onus on Reps to get it right.	Do not trust Reps' accuracy in requirements / quotes.	C —	Action Required?	→ R			
IT Developers	New advanced system. Removes difficult to maintain old system.	Skills in expert system development	None						

Figure 39 : Benjamin and Levinson Chart

It will become obvious after some initial observations and conversations where the starting position of each stakeholder is, and then you can use this table to target where you want them to be.

If you have profiled your stakeholders and mapped them as suggested in the Who Step, then use the chart to decide your starting and target positions for each stakeholder. The question, "What will it take for this stakeholder to move to the target position?" can generate some fruitful ideas that make their way into the communications plan. (See the When Step.)

26   Benjamin, R. I. and Levinson, E. (1993). "A Framework for Managing IT-Enabled Change", *Sloan Management Review*, Summer: 23-3.

Technique: The DREAM model [Change Agent]

One range of engagement is D-R-E-A-M, where we track people from initial unawareness (**Disengaged**), through initial resistance (**Resistant**), to tentative **Exploring**, to a self-aware ability to do the job (**Able**), to finally being able to **Model** and coach others.

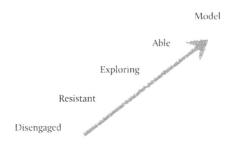

Figure 40 : The DREAM Model

People do not always start at disengaged, nor does everybody need to become a model exemplar in the change, but the range makes few assumptions and yet has simple, verifiable states along the way. For example, someone only qualifies as **Exploring**, where there is evidence that they are indeed testing matters, attempting to use new facilities, and so on. Often there are tests of competence to qualify someone as **Able**. **Model** is demonstrated by their ability to show others, coach them, or even train them.

Practice: Adjusting your engagement style [Change Agent]

As we work through the change, our engagement style itself will need to change. One useful model comes from *All Change! A Project Leader's Secret Handbook*[27]. In this, Eddie Obeng sets out a simple model of project types that has become quite widely referenced. It is so often quoted because it relates to what project managers experience.

Obeng suggests four basic types of project, and the approach to communications for the project manager should adjust accordingly:

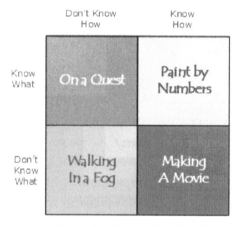

Figure 41 : Obeng's Four Quadrants

Paint by Numbers is the type of project where requirements are clear at the beginning and throughout ('We know what'), and also we have done this before, the technology is familiar ('We know how'). He calls this a 'paint by numbers' project because the management of it is rather like the children's colouring book of painting a picture with a colour code within the lines. In this case, Obeng says that the challenge of communication for a project manager is to make sure the different skills, teams and disciplines in the project each 'paint up to the lines': there are no gaps or overlaps, there is good interface management.

---

27   (Financial Times/ Prentice Hall: 1995).

Going to the left on his diagram we find the **On a Quest** type of project. Whilst there is still clarity about the requirement on this type of project, the project manager is uncertain at the beginning about how the project will deliver it. We are in foreign territory, maybe using new technologies. The name alludes to the Arthurian legend of the quest for the Holy Grail. The approach to communication here, says, Obeng, is to send your knights out exploring in different directions, get them to report back frequently, narrow down the field of search as quickly as possible, until the later stages of the project become a 'Paint by Numbers'. This has much of the approach of agile project management, although agile approaches are also applied in the remaining two contexts.

Walking in a Fog type projects appear to be the worst: we have clarity neither about where we want to be, nor how we are going to get there. It's like a group of people walking in a fog. The worst thing that can happen to the group is that they lose touch with each other on the way. Therefore frequent, close communications are necessary as we cautiously move forward. Increasingly we recognise our projects happen in a VUCA context – Volatile, Uncertain, Complex and Ambiguous.

However, Obeng submits that the most dangerous type of project is not 'Walking in a Fog', but rather **Making a Movie**. Its name alludes to a common enough experience in families: someone goes off and buys a new, creative gadget – say, a digital camcorder. They learn how to use it including all the technical functions such a sub-titling, fading in and out, and so on. Finally the day comes when the family sits down to watch the first home movie … and it's an embarrassment! It's dreadfully boring. The owner knows how to use the camera, but they realise that they are not Steven Spielberg! They don't know *what* to make a movie of, to craft a compelling cinematic sequence. This, says Obeng, is like technology-driven projects with no obvious business need. These can be dangerous and wasteful distractions. The key here is to interest the people responsible for creative content in the potential benefits of the technology, and discuss with them what might be a viable business case. Otherwise, forget the shiny new gadget.

Overall, a project might migrate from starting out as a 'Walking in a Fog'. Frequent early conversations with key stakeholders begin to dispel the mist and we move to an 'On a Quest' phase. So the nature and tempo of communications changes to more a search for the right means, the right 'how'. Ultimately, the later stages might feel like 'Paint by Numbers' for the development stakeholders, but be careful: many stakeholders in the user community will not yet have sufficient clarity on the 'how' or even 'what' questions.

The value of the Obeng model is that it helps us consciously adjust our engagement strategy, not just for different projects, but also for different phases within the same overall change.

Use these four project types to assess the degree to which you need to develop a stakeholder engagement strategy. If there is lack of clarity about the 'what' or the 'how' of the project, then communications will be a key means of managing the risk of failure.

Technique: Sequencing to Kotter's 8-Step model [Politician, Leader]

Figure 40 is a summary of another popular change model, this time from John Kotter. It is one of the most popular change models.

This one also begins by counselling against starting with a solution; instead first be urgent about why we can't stay where we are. Professor Kotter argues that such is the inertia in most organisations a change leader needs to **create a sense of urgency**. Sometimes this can be done by plainly holding up a picture of what will happen if we do nothing, a 'Do nothing vision' if you will.

1. Establish a sense of urgency

2. Create a Guiding Coalition

3. Develop a Vision and Strategy

4. Communicate the Change Vision

5. Empower people for action

6. Generate short-term wins

7. Consolidate Gains and Produce More Changes

8. Anchor New Approaches in the Culture

Figure 42 : Kotter's 8-Step Model

Power is important in change, so the next step is to **build a powerful coalition**, a group that has enough collective power to overcome the inertia and see the change through.

Clarifying that better future, explaining the reasons and benefits to be gained, is vital early work. So the next step is **Developing a Vision and Strategy**.

Kotter separates out communication into the next step: **Communicate the Change Vision**. Often change leaders will spend much time on crafting a good vision statement and a strategy, and then under-communicate them. The vision is presented, for example, at an annual conference, then maybe put on plaques around a few places and then that's it. Stakeholders forget and need the vision explained to them again; they need to be reminded.

> I cast the vision until I think people are sick of hearing it, and then they are just about getting it.
>
> — **Bill Hybels**

Empower people for action focuses on mobilising key stakeholders, often teams, to work on making the change happen.

Generate short term wins. Kotter believes demonstrable early wins are a critical success factor in most change. If you can't do this, many people will become sceptical that the change will ever win through. So a key question in this How Step is: "How can we ensure demonstrable early gains to the sceptics?"

Consolidate gains and produce more change focuses on building momentum and velocity. Agile does this through iterative development. The consolidation piece is about ensuring that the gains do not unravel, that there is some kind of incremental baseline management.

Anchor new approaches in the culture is deliberately crafting messages and events where the change that has been achieved is truly embedded, to the point that it becomes unconscious competence: "It's the way we do things around here."

So how come this book has five engagement pathway steps, and Kotter's model has eight?

Good question. Kotter's model is just one of several I recommend you consider. Remember that we are in the How Step of the engagement pathway - deciding our broad approach and the rules of engagement - and we have

"THIS IS MY 'DO NOTHING' VISION"

learned who our stakeholders are and what their attitudes, power and interests are in our initiative.

Now we need to get more specific as to what and whom we prioritise and broadly when we do this.

Kotter's model begins to break that Strategy down in a logical sequence. Along with Lewin's model and the Transition model we can use it to shape our Strategy.

Technique: Relational bank accounts [Accountant]

The 'relational bank account' is a metaphor suggested by Stephen Covey. It is simple, but has a lot of merit.

Think of a communication or conversation as a transaction where, if you offer understanding and help, you place a 'deposit' in the other person's account. Such 'deposits' might be other things, such as showing a personal interest in them, acting on your word, keeping your commitments, giving them something that is useful to them, doing them a favour, and so on.

As with any bank account, you need to make a deposit before making a withdrawal. Consider placing several such relational deposits before you think of making a withdrawal. Here a 'withdrawal' might be asking for their co operation in the change, where they might otherwise refuse.

Sales people have a similar concept in counting the number of 'touches' (contacts) with a prospect. The idea here is that given a certain number of touches, say seven, then the prospect is more likely to buy.

So consider counting the number of positive and negative contacts with each stakeholder. and then aggregating them.

Technique: The change formula [Accountant]

Beckhard and Harris[28] published this approach in 1987. For a change management model it has quite an unusual format, a mathematical formula:

$$C = [ABD] > X$$

Where

C = Change

A = Level of dissatisfaction with the status quo

B = Desirability of the proposed change or end state

D = Practicality of the change (knowledge of the next practical steps, minimal risk and disruption)

X = Perceived 'cost' of changing

Implied in the formula is the belief that if there is an absence of A, B, or D (i.e. they are at zero), then the initiative will never overcome the cost of change (resistance). Also, if the cost is perceived to be too high, stakeholders will resist the change.

Described by commentators as a concise way of capturing the dynamics of change, it is often used as a diagnostic of change readiness rather than a route map. For example, one client told me how they used the change formula in her organisation to gauge the most receptive (least resistant) business units as the best candidates for the early tranche of roll-out of a change they were introducing.

---

28   *Organizational Transitions: Managing Complex Change* (Addison-Wesley, 1987).

Practice: Defining engagement roles [Leader]

> On one change project, the CEO had a Senior VP
> leading all the consultation forums with a large
> population of stakeholders. However, for certain key,
> powerful stakeholders, it was clear that all but routine
> communications would go through the CEO; it was only
> the CEO who should talk with those powerful people.

Building on a previous practice in the Collaboration Theme ('Lead with your team'), as you discuss this with your sponsor and team, it will become clear that some people are better positioned than you are to engage with certain stakeholders. It may be, for example, that trust between these people has already been established well before you start work on this.

There may be certain types of engagement that are shared, or that are always escalated and become the responsibility of one manager.

Consider your temporary organisation. There will be key stakeholders within this (such as the Project Sponsor or Executive and the Project Office Manager), as well as key engagement roles that each should undertake. Your strategy should take this into account.

For example, in a typical project organisation might look something like this:

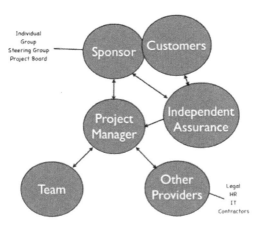

Figure 43 : A typical project organisation

Sponsor. Consider these roles for your sponsor:

- Delivering keynote messages at large forums.
- Engaging powerful, key stakeholders one-on-one.

The sponsor should include one or more key representatives of operational stakeholders (customer), people who will have to live with and use the outputs after the project is finished.

Project Manager. The project manager is usually the coordinator and leader of the whole engagement campaign, facilitator of workshops, and responsible for planning and tracking the engagements.

Project Assurance. Assurance roles are valuable in providing independent monitoring of stakeholder engagement, effectiveness of communications and of stakeholder satisfaction.

Team Managers. These roles can be delegated communications matters of a more routine nature, and provide the others in the team with help in communications effort, managing and tracking written communications and forums, and key milestones.

It usually rests with the team leader to ensure good communications links are established across the organisation, upwards and downwards, and often links with those outside the organisation, such as key clients or suppliers. Project teams, in particular, may span several business units, and must work effectively at the interfaces with these units, being prepared to work across boundaries.

There is a strong move in many progressive organisations towards agile, self-directed teams (see the Agile chapter). However, such teams still need to attend to links with other teams and other parts of the wider organisation in order to be at their most effective.

Practice: Modelling the change you want to lead [Leader]

> Nothing sends a more powerful message about what is really important to your team than WHERE you spend your time. If your time is spent on the front lines with customers, then customers are most important. If your time is spent face to face with your R&D team, then R&D is what is most important.
>
> **—Doug Hall**

One of the most effective influencing strategies is this one illustrated by Jimmy Carter.

> President Carter, after leaving office, went on to devote much his time to promoting the work of Habitat for Humanity, a charity that mobilises volunteers to build homes for the poor.
>
> It was his practice, whenever invited to speak of this work on TV, to arrive dressed in work clothes, with a belt of tools around his waist. It sent out a powerful message: that Carter 'walked the talk', that there was an urgent job to be done, and if a president can do, I can too.

As you begin to experience the change for yourself, you will identify issues and challenges that you might otherwise have overlooked. This is important experience that needs to be factored into other practices and techniques, such as force field analysis. This will help you develop a richer and more robust strategy.

So consider how you might lead by example for your change. Could you become one of the 'early adopters' and show people what the change would be like and feel like when they meet with you?

The opposite can risk a crisis of credibility: if you do not adopt the change early, then others will wonder why, and whether you believe in it yourself.

Engaging with suppliers

An approach all too common is to bully suppliers into delivering on time and to cost. As a supplier myself I have been on the receiving end of this sort of practice. The approach is to view the supplier as a stakeholder to whom you can transfer not just risk, but also stress. Doing this has a pay-off in the short term in that the supplier seems to jump, and I suppose it can feel briefly cathartic. But it usually fails long-term.

Also, procurement practices have increasingly veered to excluding all else but the lowest price solutions, which in turn has positioned all supply as a commodity. Suppliers, though, are often there to deliver a service that cannot and should not be commoditised for the customer.

Brian Wernham[29] argues for contract structures that pay by short increments of value delivered, where the customer is not locked in for long periods to unproductive relationships with suppliers.

The working relationship between customers and suppliers can be within a framework of value delivery. In these cases, the customer does not delude themselves that they can transfer all risk to the supplier. Once the customer recognises that not all risk can be tossed over the contract 'wall' to the supplier, then the customer can work to optimum engagement in such an agile contract structure shoulder-to-shoulder with the supplier, where both customer and supplier look at the problem together as business partners. The supplier is incentivised to drive up demonstrable value, because they will retain the contract longer and will be appropriately rewarded. The customer shows that they will not abdicate ownership of all the risks and so will seek to remove obstacles to the supplier in driving up that value.

We need to learn to shape contract structures more creatively and lead suppliers much more progressively.

---

29   Wernham, op. cit.

How risk relates to stakeholders and benefits [Speculator]

Risk, stakeholders and benefits are each interconnected, as Figure 44 shows:

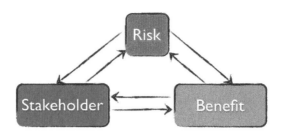

Figure 44 : The relationships between risks, benefits and stakeholders

A risk is perceived as such by stakeholders. However, each stakeholder will perceive different risks from their own perspective. As we saw, with the benefits distribution table, there will be a different mix of benefits and dis-benefits for each stakeholder. Finally, there will be risks to each benefit being realised, which could be because of some of your stakeholders.

So the triad of risk, stakeholders and benefits are very closely related to each other. Thinking like a speculator will involve generating engagement options and different goals that will factor different balances in all three.

> Several doctors in a hospital fear that they will have less discretion in how they use their time when a new paging system is introduced. However, in other hospitals where it is used, the paging system allows doctors to avoid wasting significant time on unnecessary checking in/out procedures thus freeing up more time and discretion for their clinical work. But if this is not explained to them clearly and persuasively early on, their growing resistance could threaten the success of the whole change.

Practice: Compiling an engagement strategy document [Leader, Accountant]

> Thoughts disentangle themselves when
> they pass through your fingertips.
>
> **—Dawson Trotman**

I'm not an advocate of reams of documentation. Nevertheless, I concede that documentation does have its place. The act of writing something down clarifies the mind. If you are leading engagement collaboratively, certain agreements must be written to prevent ambiguity and clarify decisions later. So I favour an agile "just enough documentation" (JED). In pulling all your thinking in the How Step together, I recommend you write an engagement strategy.

Items in such a strategy might cover:

- A **list of all the stakeholders**, supplemented with a stakeholder map or mind map

- **Analyses of stakeholders**, such as the influence-impact grid and empathy maps

- **Prioritisation** of stakeholders to be engaged

- The **approaches and mechanisms** of engagement, possibly broken down by particular segments or categories of stakeholder

- **Roles** in engagement. Who does what in proactive engagement, the roles within the change team

- **Measures of effectiveness**, both in terms of communications and positions of the stakeholders.

The strategic "No" [Leader]

I have written elsewhere about the chronic illness of 'hurry sickness'[30]. It has its root in an excessive busyness that comes out of our inability to say, "No" to many requests and opportunities that come our way.

So how do you know when to say, "No"? One answer comes from the work you do in shaping your Strategy. Strategy is more than just shaping the game plan and laying out the rules of engagement. A good strategy helps you focus your effort, to prioritise, to stay within your limits or margins. A good strategy helps you to know when to say, "No." Consider this story:

> In the example earlier, of the roll-out of a new business model to various country offices, the strategic approach prioritised offices in terms of the Change Formula. The thinking here was that we need early victories, and this was more likely to be found from the more change-ready offices.

> Suppose that, early on in the programme, the country director for, say, Italy, argued forcefully that his office should be next in line for the switch over, and that he had appealed first to your Sponsor. From your briefing you suspect his agenda is more to do with fast-tracking his career than for any relative merits of the Italian office. You re-assess its readiness and find that, if anything, there are still greater transition risks for that office. What should you do?

With no pre-agreed strategy with your Sponsor, how could you have decided on this matter? Political power and enthusiasm could persuade you to overload your change programme. You would be busier, and over-stretched, without needing to be that vulnerable.

---

30   See http://practicebites.com/hurry-sickness .

Technique: Review & revise your strategy [Accountant]

"How can they tell?"

—Dorothy Parker

on hearing of the death of President Calvin Coolidge (aka 'Silent Cal')

Having attempted many or all of the above practices and techniques stand back from your strategy and see if it all hangs together, whether it all is internally consistent and coherent. Particularly look for any potential to increase confusion. A good strategy should work to reduce confusion.

So, consider how your whole game plan works from the perspective of your team, each stakeholder and the overall 'story'.

1. Clarity of roles is crucial. Does everyone understand what they and everyone else in the team is supposed to do and their other responsibilities?

2. Provide for two-way communications. How is feedback going to be dealt with, responded to, and how quickly?

3. Cherry pick. Use what you find useful or that appears essential. Feel free to discard elements that do not appear to be relevant to your brief.

4. How will you know the strategy is working? For example,

    »   Are there particular target positions some stakeholders must reach?

    »   How will you know if you are under or over-communicating? If you over-communicate, you run the risk of defeating your own communication aims by being dismissed as 'noise'.

    »   Miscommunication? Is the timing, format or content of your communications confusing?

» Non-communication? Are you missing an opportunity to converse with someone?

5. Consider also identifying individuals among groups of stakeholders that you could use to act as **listening posts**, people who have their ear to the ground, and who would give you accurate, honest feedback on how news and developments are being viewed.

6. Above all, beware of making stakeholder engagement into an industry at the expense of developing constructive relationships with your stakeholders.

It is useful in this practice to bring in a friendly critic from outside the team, a Devil's Advocate. Often larger organisations have a specialist in this area that can add huge value by assuring your approach.

Living the principles in the How Step

Seek first to understand, and then be understood: You will find that the techniques of customer segmentation and working on value propositions develops a deeper understanding of your stakeholders. Discussions on slack, checking the current positions of some stakeholders, testing change readiness and the reasons for it, understanding the risks to stakeholders, all live this principle.

Effective change is always led: Shaping the engagement strategy is very much the domain of leadership. Leading people is more than just gaining clarity about the desired future, but it is also about being clear about the journey, and the stages in that journey.

Habits are the inhibitors and the goal: The change formula recognises the very real inertia in an organisation that must be overcome to make a successful change happen. This is illustrative of a number of change management models that you could shape your engagement around, several of which recognise the power of existing habits as well as the need to embed new ones. In particular, at a business unit level, the transition planning model makes this very clear. In this way, using such a change management model at the heart of your engagement strategy will help you live this principle. At the individual level, the restraining forces on your stakeholders can be identified here, which are often manifested as habits.

Recognise and minimise the pain of change: Value propositions and empathy maps can tease out where current pain exists for some stakeholders. The discussion on force field analysis, in particular Schein's analysis of how this plays out in the individual, helps identify areas of pain in the change itself, and help to minimise these, leading on to transition planning. Also tracking emotional states, devising support through these, as well as reviewing currents levels of slack and change readiness, and adjusting style of messaging through the engagement, each in different ways help you practice this principle. Pitches help clarify and minimise the uncertainty and the fear that goes with that of your proposed change. Minimising the confusion (pain) of mixed messages is a central purpose of the engagement strategy. Finally, attention to the stress-recovery cycles involved in people changing, and working with these, will help you minimise the pain for these stakeholders.

High performance comes through people and action: Leading with your team by giving clarity of the engagement roles within that team will help you live this principle in this step.

Integrity is powerfully persuasive: The review and revise practice towards the end of this chapter will help ensure that there is internal integrity within your strategy. Leading by modelling the change is also operating in integrity.

Feelings trump reason, and meaning trumps authority: Emotions are recognised in several practices and techniques, such as the Kubler-Ross model, in this step. The value propositions technique places a premium on clearly identifying the benefits to stakeholders and the reasons for them to believe you. The bank of pitches are essentially about finding creative ways of mobilising the meaning of the change.

When to use this Step

- Before your change initiative even begins

- You discover excessive apathy or denial among certain stakeholders whom you need to influence

- There are indicators that your change is not working or not gaining enough traction

- Some people are still confused by your messages or say that some of them contradict what others are saying

- At the end of every phase of your engagement as laid out in your strategy and plan.

The How Step - Summary

- Decide your overall strategy before you plan specific engagement events (How before When)

- Different stakeholders require different approaches; one size does not fit all, so segment them further

- Consider what is valuable to your stakeholders

- Assemble a bank of pitches

- Consider the forces at work on groups and individuals relating to your proposed change, and consider ways of weakening the resisting forces

- Allow for the 'performance dip' in transition and begin setting expectations

- Consider the current and your desired target positions for each stakeholder

- Engage as a team; consider roles for engagement within your team

- Change strategies usually follow one or more change models; these help set out the broad story of change that your stakeholders will go through

- People adopt a new innovation at different points; consider using the Innovation Curve as part of your story

- People go through a series of predictable emotions when confronted with an unwelcome, inevitable change; consider using the Kubler-Ross curve as a way of shaping the sequence of engagement; also consider using the Bridges model

- Consider where power really lies among your stakeholders: it is never distributed evenly

- Consider shaping your engagement with some stakeholders as a series of deposits and withdrawals from a relational bank account, making sure you are never in deficit

- Consciously adjust your communications style as you go through different phases of a longer programme or project

- Pull it all together: having attempted many or all of the above, stand back from your strategy and see if it all hangs together.

How Practices

- Prioritising by innovation adoption

- Tracking emotional states

- Leading with the Bridges' transition model

- Monitoring and providing slack

- Monitoring energy and planning recovery

- Targeting positions

- Adjusting your engagement style

- Defining engagement roles

- Modelling the change you want to lead

- Compiling an engagement strategy document.

How Techniques

- Customer segmentation

- Crafting value propositions

- Assembling a bank of pitches

- Force field analysis

- The individual's force field

- Transition planning

- The DREAM model

- Sequencing to the Kotter 8-step model

- Relational bank accounts

- The change formula

- Review and revise your strategy.

CHAPTER 11

The When Step: Planning your messages

In the previous chapter we looked at shaping your engagement. Deliberately, this did not commit to specific dates and times. Now we look at planning your engagement. Your plan will take account of particular events in your change initiative, which will affect the exact timing of engagement events.

The plan sets out how, where and when you and your team will engage with people during the course of your change. As a plan, it allows you to control different people's contributions and keep the whole communications effort coordinated.

A common risk is that the very people you are seeking to influence will receive mixed messages. What follows from that is confusion at least, resistance at worst, which a good communications plan helps avoid.

Practice: Writing a communications plan [Accountant]

The essential components of a communications plan are very simple:

Business Context. The plan may be read by a future team member with only partial briefing or understanding of the background, history and context of the change, the key issues and people involved. It may be read in isolation from other documentation, so this section helps if it reads as a stand-alone document.

Opinion Environment. Are opinions towards the change positive or negative? Is there 'change fatigue'? How successful have recent changes been as experienced by this group? What is the change readiness of the group?

Target Audience. This gives a brief profile of the target audience, their aspirations and fears, their demography, needs and attitudes. Sometimes it is useful to structure the Communications Plan by different audiences.

Key Messages. Consider a one-sentence 'Point of View' that you want to get across clearly; supplement this by what actions, if any, you want the audience to take, and define three key benefits to them if they do. Key messages must be consistent from whoever gives them in the change team.

Objectives. What you want to achieve through this engagement? What is the intended result?

Channels and Tools. Which medium or media will you use to reach your objectives? What communications technologies will you employ and why?

Resources. How much money, people and technology will this all require? Remember, most organisations under-communicate change because of lack of resources.

Timing. Are there key planned events in the transition (e.g. launch date)? Are there key events to monitor that will trigger communications (e.g. early success stories)? Is there a rhythm to the communications? Are there agreed service level response times to feedback from stakeholders?

Responsibilities. Who does what in the communications campaign? This should be consistent with the Engagement Strategy (See the 'How' activity). Remember, you do not need to do this all on your own; you can delegate.

Use the following questions to develop your Communications Plan.

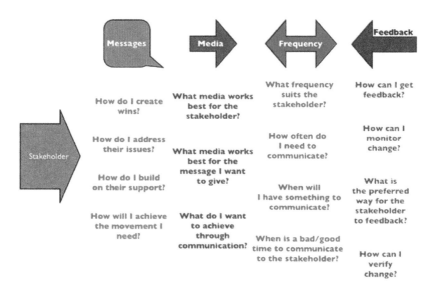

Source: Adapted from Mark Withers, Mightywaters

Figure 45 : Questions to develop your Communications Plan

The 'how' questions under 'Messages' should be addressed in your Stakeholder Engagement Strategy, leaving your Communications Plan free to be re-worked independently.

Practice: Using the right medium [Marketer]

The medium is the message.

—Marshall McLuhan

A common mistake is to attempt to engage all stakeholders using the same medium; worst of all, choosing email to be that medium.

Some media are great for informing people. Some are much better at influencing them. Consider this diagram:

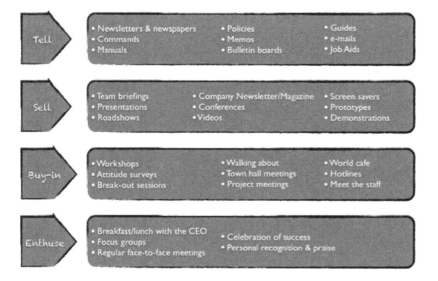

Figure 46 : Communication objectives and media

Use this diagram as a guide. Notice the modes tend to change from written (at the top) to face-to-face (at the bottom)[1].

Note: this is not an exhaustive list of available media; it can't be – new channels are becoming available to us all the time; e.g. Facebook, YouTube, Twitter, internal wikis, etc.

---

1   See 'The science of face time' below.

Ask stakeholders, or representatives of groups, for their preferred media, and how often they would like to be contacted. You are attempting to make the whole experience of being contacted by you and your team as friendly and as sensitive as possible. Consider this part of your influencing strategy.

How about abuses of these media? For example, most people learn very quickly that email is not the best medium for conveying disapproval or anger to someone. Most of us have done this, with the consequences of a damaged relationship or even the matter spiraling into what have been called 'flame wars'.

There is an opposite abuse of media. Consider this all-too-familiar scene:

> You attend a conference, and you are very much looking forward to hearing one particular speaker's views on a subject. You gather with about 250 other intelligent people, whereupon the speaker reads out their paper to you word for word. No value-added opinions or advice are offered, just what is in the paper or what is on the screen. You and the rest of the audience could have read the paper for yourselves or got the PowerPoint on Slideshare.

I am amazed at how this still seems to be tolerated as acceptable practice all across the world, particularly within academic circles. Why do we put up with it? The speaker could have expressed their opinions and point of view with passion, and could have called people to action[2]. Instead they droned on, probably with the support of far too many PowerPoint slides[3], most of which had words the speaker read out to you. What a missed opportunity! What an abuse of the medium![4]

As a general rule, if you use face-to-face modes of engagement then your objective is to influence, to gain opinions, to make a call to action. If your objective is to inform then you can use static written material, whether electronic or hard copy.

---

2   See Bert Decker's work, for example, as an excellent corrective to passionless, pointless presentations.

3   If you want to improve your use of visual media using tools such as PowerPoint or Keynote, then I would recommend Garr Reynolds' *Presentation Zen*, or Nancy Duarte's *Slide:ology*.

4   Note to reader: Did you notice with this rant that I'm not following my own advice here? I'm abusing a written medium to express negative passion. (My apologies, but it felt good.)

Technique: Test the signal to noise ratio [Change Agent]

Everybody's talkin' at me,

I don't hear a word they're sayin'...

—Harry Nilsson (Lyrics to Midnight Cowboy[5])

Telecommunications engineers use a measure called the 'Signal to Noise Ratio'. In order for a signal to be received clearly over a line, the clarity of signal compared to the other noise on the line is critical to the message being received. There will always be noise on the line; the issue is how clear is the message compared to that background noise. Noise is part of the Shannon and Weaver model of communication[6].

If you carry that concept over into the workplace you will identify all kinds of 'noise' that competes for people's attention: their general busyness with other matters, urgent meetings, volumes of emails being received, rumours, gossip, and all the other campaigns, projects and initiatives competing for their limited attention.

Wikipedia lists:

1. Environmental noise, e.g. standing next to loudspeakers at a party.

2. Physiological-impairment noise, e.g. tinnitus (ringing in the ears).

3. Semantic noise: different interpretations of the same word, e.g. 'weed' as an undesirable plant or as a euphemism for marijuana.

4. Syntactical noise: mistakes in grammar, such as an abrupt change in verb tense during a sentence.

5. Organisational noise: for example, unclear or badly stated directions.

6. Cultural noise: stereotypical assumptions, such as offending a non-Christian by wishing them "Merry Christmas."

---

5   Writer Fred Neil.
6   Shannon, Claude E. & Warren Weaver (1949): *A Mathematical Model of Communication*. Urbana, IL: University of Illinois Press

7. Psychological noise: where certain attitudes make communication difficult. For instance, great sadness may cause someone to lose focus on the present moment.

At this point in your planning, it might be very helpful to have a session with the team to explore this. To practice this technique, run through these questions with your team:

- What are certain stakeholders actually hearing? Is it different from what you intended?

- Why should these stakeholder pay attention to your initiative and its signals rather than to something else?

- Is there anything stopping them from just ignoring your message and giving their scarce attention to something else?

- How are you earning the right to be heard?

Don't limit your efforts merely to amplifying or boosting your signal; you should consider first how you could reduce the noise. For example, people often find off-site events very helpful for this very reason, so that people can give their full attention to your messages and requests.

Also, use the Adapt Step to gain valuable information on the clarity of the messages you have given out. How? Just ask people what they think was said.

Technique: The SUCCESs framework [Leader]

The Heath brothers, in their earlier book *Made to Stick*[7], presented a very simple acronym (SUCCESs) for creating compelling, 'sticky' (memorable) messages. This is a useful structure in communications planning generally:

Simple. Messages need to be simple. They say this is not to dumb them down, but is about prioritising what is of first importance in the message. What is core?

Unexpected. To get attention violate some conventional wisdom. ("Don't use us if you....") Or use curiosity. ("Which is really more deadly: Jaws or Bambi?")[8] Before your message will stick, your audience has to want it.

---

7   *Made to Stick: why some ideas take hold and others come unstuck* (Arrow, 2008). I find the Heath brothers have a gift for making ideas accessible. They practice what they preach.
8   It's Bambi... Read their book!

Concrete. Use concrete, sensory language, however abstract your message might be. It uses the Velcro theory of memory: the more sensory hooks you can use, the more likely it is to stick.

Credible. Credibility comes from outside authorities, or from within using human-scale statistics. ("If a million people were an inch high, then the population of the UK would be taller than 19 out of twenty people.") Let people try before you buy. (Use showrooms, laboratories, play areas.)

Emotional. People don't care so much about numbers as they do about people; which is why disaster appeals often focus on one person or family, and make the appeal about helping them. Remember "WIIFM" (What's in it for me?). Identifying with real people often trumps over self-interest and reason. Note Kotter's position illustrated in Principle 7: Feelings trump reason.

Stories. Again, the power of stories is through simulation, empathy and inspiration. Good stories seem to have a universal appeal, so use them.

Practice: Mining and mobilising your project collateral [Accountant]

If you use some standard method or Body of Knowledge (such as the APM's Body of Knowledge or PMI's PMBoK) then you will be assembling a wealth of material that you could share with stakeholders. Consider the existing documents produced and maintained by your team; how might you use these, or elements of them, to aid engagement with your stakeholders? You might have many of the following:

- Programme/Project Vision
- Project Charter or Brief
- Project Initiation Document (PID)
- Business Case
- Prototypes
- Project Plan
- Product Descriptions or User Stories
- Highlight Reports
- Burn-down chart

- Issues Register or Log

- Risk Register entries

- End Stage Reports

- Closure Report

- Gateway Review Report.

Of course there is a serious danger that comes with all methods: blindly following them, and generating masses of documentation, purely because the method says so. It can become a self-serving industry.

Regarding the specific case of a **plan**, though, it is worth remembering that it has at least three common uses, albeit complementary ones:

1. As a vehicle to **consider** future actions, helping the planner to think things through in advance. The very act of planning is clarifying for the planner.

2. As a means to **communicate** and gain commitment from decision-makers and the rest of the team.

3. As means of tracking and so being able to **control** the project as it is being executed.

Also, the **business case** should not be confined to merely justifying the change for approval or for funds. A simple précis of it can communicate the purpose and importance to other stakeholders. It is an ongoing means of focusing your team and other stakeholders throughout your project. No doubt, you will need to paraphrase and shorten the business case for most audiences, but it is still the heartbeat of your change[9].

Project managers often forget that much feedback can be gleaned from certain stakeholders through their **Issues Register** or Log. Used in this way, the Issues Register becomes a sort of project 'suggestions box.'

---

9   This is relevant to the *Bank of Pitches* in the How Step.

Practice: Influencing through others [Politician]

Several research studies have shown a striking pattern: people need to hear about change from two key sources – the **most senior person involved** in the change and their **line manager**. The senior manager is the most convincing about the business messages including the reasons for the change, whereas the line manager is best for communicating the personal messages, contextualising it into the day-to-day, explaining exactly what the practical implications might be for the individual. People appreciate hearing about the strategic drivers for a change, whilst at the same time having it contextualised into what it means for them in more concrete terms.

Often the sequence in which we influence people is crucial. With the Innovation Adoption Model[10], for example, it is important that we prioritise the Early Adopters, as these are the Opinion Leaders. In smaller groups use the power mapping technique to identify who should be approached first.

In command-and-control cultures, it is important to gain permission from more senior people before approaching their direct reports. If that is the culture you are working within, make sure you respect that etiquette.

Practice: Engaging your gatekeepers early [Politician]

> No tyranny is so irksome as petty tyranny:
> the officious demands of policemen,
> government clerks, and electromechanical gadgets.
>
> **— Edward Abbey**

There is a certain category of stakeholder that we might call the 'gatekeepers': people who hold power over your progress but are external to it, people such as quality managers, contract managers, auditors, town planners[11], procurement managers, and so on. All such bureaucrats exercise power as gatekeepers, the power to say 'No', the power not to let something pass through the gate.

---

10   See the How Step.
11   I write from my own experience as a recovering town planner.

I have found that one of the best ways to engage gatekeepers is to seek them out first and ask their advice before you need their approval. If they have a policing role, they are more likely to give those who do not consult them a harder time.

Cynical? I don't think I so; it's merely working with human nature. Is there a risk in consulting them like this? Of course, but I've found it invariably works, and works well.

So consider scheduling early contact with gatekeepers wherever you identify them.

Practice: Varying the engagement tempo [Marketer]

Often we plan a fairly constant pace of things. To your stakeholder community this can become fairly monotonous and they can switch off.

Often tempo needs to be varied, particularly in the case of roll-outs, or other kinds of similar deployment. Most people learn to plan the earlier phases of commissioning to last longer. The pace picks up as most of the major lessons have been learned from the first few roll-outs. So expect the early roll-outs to take rather longer.

> Rick Warren tells[12] of the time he was invited with a number of others to visit the Dreamworks studio to be consulted on the script for the feature-length cartoon that was later released as *The Prince of Egypt*. He was intrigued by the storyboard that was spread along the wall of a long corridor. He asked what the two curves were running along the storyboard. One of them was the emotional curve, which had nine peaks and troughs. He was told that it is important not to keep an audience at a positive or negative pitch for long stretches, so the story was crafted with an emotional rhythm that was reinforced by the colours used in the different scenes: light pastels for the positive scenes, and dark reds and

---

12   From a talk I heard Warren gave at a Leadership Conference.

browns for the emotionally negative scenes. Keeping people at the same emotional pace is not as engaging and entertaining, he was told, as a story that is played out with some emotional rhythm.

Practice: Timing your messages [Marketer]

There is a tide in the affairs of men,
which, taken at the flood, leads on to fortune.

—Shakespeare (Julius Caesar, Act IV)

Consider the following when planning communications:

- Are we ready to communicate 'early wins'?

- When is a good time to communicate with *this* stakeholder? When is it a bad time?

- Is there a pace and rhythm to our communications?

- What is the maximum period we will budget before getting back to each stakeholder?

A public relations consultant once told me that we always need to ask, "Is this of interest to the market and to our customers?" The answer was 'yes' rather more often than I had expected.

Consider for a moment, those times when matters are so pressing that you regard any other interruption as unwelcome. How could you make sure you are still reacting appropriately when you find yourself interrupted by someone, when you are fully engaged on something important? How can you make sure you don't inflict this kind of stress on your busy stakeholders?

The balance is then:

- Knowing when you have something worth telling that party

- Knowing when they are likely to be most receptive

- Combining the news and the receptive moment to the maximum effect.

Technique: Track stakeholders across the radar [Change Agent, Accountant]

Of course, stakeholder positions are dynamic through the life of your engagement. In the Who Step we introduced the Stakeholder Radar technique. Here is how the radar can change through time, rather like the radar in a control tower tracking an incoming aircraft:

Figure 47 : Tracking a stakeholder across the radar

This illustrates the importance of maintaining the connections between several of these techniques. Stakeholder positions will and should change. And so we need to adjust our engagement accordingly. Try including snapshots of stakeholder positions in the radar in your communications plan.

Practice: Pursuing clarity and driving out ambiguity [Leader]

There is a risk of a crucial loss of credibility in engagement. It is confusion. Our messages must be crafted in a way that is clear to each audience. There are some sobering challenges when it comes to clarity.

For example, Professor Howard Gardner of Harvard argues that when an audience is heterogeneous (mixed) it is likely that you need to communicate at the level of a nine-year-old. This sounds extreme but it has been tested. So if you have groups present in a conference representing different stakeholders, jargon will not work. The language needs to be simple and accessible. If people do not understand, at best they will miss the message and switch off, at worst they get annoyed or even angry.

A dangerous failure of clarity can be ambiguity. It is wise to get communiqués of a particularly sensitive nature reviewed by a friendly reviewer outside of your team, preferably with some familiarity of the target audience.

Napoleon's Fool

> The story goes[13] that Napoleon once encountered a man who could be relied on to take the wrong interpretation of anything said or written. Most were impatient with this man, regarding him as a fool. With his genius, however, the emperor saw a great value in this. In fact he regarded it as a rare gift.
>
> So he employed this man to stay at his side during military campaigns. During the heat of battle he would scribble a message to one of his Marshals and pass it to the Fool, asking him what he thought it meant. If there was any ambiguity, the man would find it, and Napoleon would rewrite the order until his Fool landed on the correct interpretation, thereby avoiding a potentially fatal risk that his orders would be misinterpreted.

---

13   I have been unable to validate or source this delightful story; even if it's a myth, it still makes a valid point.

In the light of this story, do you make the best use of people with specialist communications skills - not fools - within your organisation? For example, some have a press office. Others have public relations specialists. These experienced people can be given a role (see the chapter on the "How" step) in checking certain messages for clarity before they are released.

Practice: Planning interviews [Change Agent]

Your communications plan will almost certainly include several one-on-one interviews. These are often critical. I find this short checklist[14] helpful when planning an interview:

1.   Set aside at least 45 minutes for each interview.

2.   Limit an interview to just three or four major topics.

3.   Explore in conversation matters of culture, their challenges, and their goals and aspirations rather than features.

4.   Be prepared for each interview.

5.   Let interviewees know in advance what you'll ask them.

6.   Explain that you will be taking notes and why.

7.   Don't be afraid to ask one interviewee to comment on something another interviewee said (as long as the other party didn't say it in confidence) using your tact.

8.   There are no correct number of interviews.

9.   If necessary, ask an interviewee to wait while you make a note.

10. Decide for yourself whether you'll record interviews.

---

14   Abridged from: UX Matters Blog (www.uxmatters.com), 10th September 2007

Practice: Creating feedback and response systems [Accountant]

As stressed earlier, a common missing element in communications planning is allowing for the two-way flow of communications. Your stakeholders need to be provided with the means to get back to you and your team, and you need to give visible signals that you are hearing and responding. Without this, you are not engaging, you are merely broadcasting. Note, for example, the discussion earlier about using the Issues Register; but this is only a partial answer.

Many organisations now have intranet systems, such as Sharepoint or Yammer. You can use such vehicles to manage feedback needs, but they need to be backed up with a clear plan on how the system will be moderated and administered, otherwise it risks becoming a distraction and a drain on the team's time.

> One of my clients on a change management course shared with me a remarkable initiative within her organisation, the Cambridgeshire Constabulary[15], the regional police force for that part of England, called Rumour Mill.
>
> Rumour Mill is, in essence, very simple. It is an Intranet discussion board, where anyone can post any question or comment about current happenings within the force ... anonymously.
>
> Let the radical transparency of this sink in for a moment ... anyone ... anonymously ... on anything! Could your organisation cope with that? Would your leaders be courageous enough to provide and promote such a forum?
>
> So, if someone - anyone - posts a comment such as, "This initiative will mean the loss of twenty jobs at HQ", within a couple of hours at most a response is posted by the change team, correcting any wrong assumptions or clarifying any confusion where appropriate.

---

15   Used with the kind permission of the Cambridgeshire Constabulary.

> People following the thread can see the openness
> of leadership here and the abiding trust grows that
> everyone is being heard.

Stephen Denning[16] advocates such radical transparency. I can see how courageous and powerful this is. All credit to Cambridgeshire.

Living the principles in the When Step

Seek first to understand and then be understood: As you move towards planning specific communication events, issues of media and timing require of you a deeper level of understanding of your stakeholders. Again, one of the simplest ways is to ask them. The search for avoiding confusion, and pursuing clarity is also living this principle.

Effective change is always led: Planning interviews as well as engaging gatekeepers early are leadership behaviours. To do these well you must have clarity in your own mind of what outcome you want; which is thinking like a leader. Mobilising the right people, such as line managers, to engage with others is also a leadership strategy.

Habits are the inhibitors and the goal: Well timed reminders will help certain stakeholders develop healthy new habits. Timely communication of early wins will encourage others to believe in your change and begin the difficult process of learning new habits.

Recognise and minimise the pain of change: In some working environments, just paying attention to yet another change initiative is painful for some stakeholders; it is seen as adding to their noise, a distraction. With some careful planning, you can avoid provoking unnecessary resistance to your messages.

High performance comes through people and action: Planning often leads people to action, and in this case to engagement. However, you need to guard against paralysis by analysis. Don't let the good feeling of fashioning a great plan deceive you that the job is nearly done. It isn't.

---

16   *The Leader's Guide to Radical Management* (2010). It's his fifth principle of continuous innovation.

However, to create the best of engagement plans does require talking with stakeholders. Asking representative stakeholders how and when they would like to receive messages from the initiative is a kind of engagement in and of itself. Also, a good plan should keep you accountable to act on it.

Integrity is powerfully persuasive: Making the whole communications piece as stakeholder-friendly as possible is showing you care. Asking stakeholders how they would like to interact with you during the journey is showing you are prepared to serve them. Being as clear as you can be about the business drivers for your change is also walking in integrity.

Feelings trump reason, and meaning trumps authority: Using the appropriate media to conveying feelings is crucial. More collaborative and two-way media will achieve the heart-to-heart exchanges leaving all parties feeling respected. Meaning will come from the most senior person in the change as well as from the individual's line manager.

When to take this Step

- When you have a rough strategy established

- At the end of every phase of your engagement as laid out in your strategy and plan. Consider planning as iterative

- A new channel or medium becomes available to you and your stakeholder community. For example, your organisation might introduce something like Yammer part-way through your change

- You have appropriate success stories, early wins. You need to tell people

- There are signs of burnout among some of your stakeholders

- Evidence that people are still unaware of your change, or are not reaching their planned target.

When Step - Summary

- A communications plan helps you reduce the risk of people being confused, of receiving mixed messages

- Always allow for two-way communication in your plan

- Use the right medium for your aim; note the growing body of research about the importance of 'face-to-face'

- Avoid an over-reliance on email and other text-only media

- Exploit your existing project documents for key messages

- Seek out the 'gatekeepers' early. Ask them for advice

- Make sure the right people are influencing each stakeholder: the most senior person and their line manager

- Make sure communications are planned with a consideration of timing and rhythm

- Drive out ambiguity in your messages, getting others to check before issuing

- Where meeting one-on-one, always plan

- Provide adequate feedback and response systems.

When Practices

- Writing a communications plan

- Using the right medium

- Mining and mobilise=ing your project collateral

- Influencing through others

- Engaging your gatekeepers early

- Varying the engagement tempo

- Timing your messages

- Pursuing clarity and driving out ambiguity

- Planning interviews

- Creating feedback and response systems.

When Techniques

- Test the signal to noise ratio

- The SUCCESs framework

- Track stakeholders across the radar.

CHAPTER 12

The Engage Step: Doing it

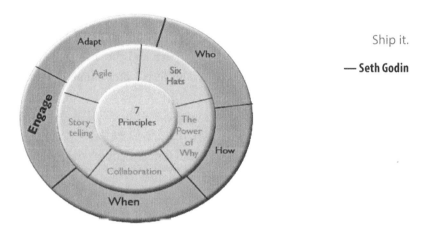

Ship it.

— Seth Godin

N ow you must step out and do it.

Management literature, if anything, errs on the side of analysis, planning and strategising. Yet nothing has been achieved in this world without plain old-fashioned execution. The iterative development approach of Agile - doing a bit then using the feedback to correct and steer the next bit, and keeping on doing that - places execution at the centre of it all. This is a good model for applying the engagement pathway. Use the Engage Step frequently.

Much of the best management practice I and my colleagues have worked on with our clients - methods and frameworks such as PRINCE2 project management, MSP® programme management, M_o_R® management of risk, and so on - were originally developed to help execution. The tragic paradox is that much of the use of these that we see majors on analysis, not execution. We have seen organisations adopt these best management practices and turn them into an obsession with governance, planning and reporting, with an emphasis on process and documentation. But where is the execution?

> Plans are only good intentions unless they
> immediately degenerate into hard work.

—Peter F. Drucker

Recent research has shown that all entrepreneurs have a proclivity to action. Schlesinger[1] and colleagues argue that the mantra for would-be entrepreneurs is "Action Trumps Everything". They stress that this is not reckless, but is considered risk-taking in the relentless pursuit of taking the next step.

I would go so far as to say that **this is the most important Step of the whole engagement pathway**. Neglect this Step and you are likely to achieve nothing. Conversely, even if you do only this Step, with caution and remaining alert, and it will take you a long way.

Practice: Prioritising your time [Leader]

An email Inbox is other people's to do list for you.

—Anon

Take out your calendar, diary, time sheet or record log if you have one, and look at how you spent your working time over the last few weeks. Think about the balance of your time spent in different types of activities on the project. How much of it has been spent in conversations with people? Please try it. You will get more value from this book if you do.

Ignore emailing; that doesn't usually count. Dealing with email usually becomes a matter of merely processing information and of keeping on top of one's inbox. As one of my reviewers commented, emailing usually reverts to little more than 'message management.'

How much time do you really spend talking with people in and around your initiative? If you are like me, you probably can't tell exactly from what you can recall and from what is in your diary. So try keeping a record over the next week. Log your time into different categories and track in 15-minute blocks. Then at the end of the week work out the proportion of your time you spent in relationship with people.

1   *Just Start: Take Action, Embrace Uncertainty, Create the Future* (Harvard Business Press: 2012)

Below is an example weekly time log you can use for this. Our research has shown that high performers have a strong relational leaning; that is to say, the higher-performers spent more of their discretionary time in conversations with people than the rest of us. The difference is quite marked: 40-80% compared with perhaps only 10% for the majority.

Where are you on this scale? How can you change that for the better?

Activity No.	Activity	Hours
1	Emailing responses	
2	Writing reports or other project documentation	
3	Creating or reviewing plans	
4	Pro-active work (Designing or building solutions)	
5	Routine progress meetings	
6	Training	
7	Travelling	
8	One-to-one conversations (initiated by me)	
9	One-to-one conversations (initiated by others)	
10	Telephone calls (self-initiated)	
11	Answering telephone calls	
12	Research (e.g. browsing the web)	
13	Meetings with intent to reach specific agreements or make specific decisions	
14	Meetings that form part of your Communications Plan	
	Total	
	1. Total the hours	
	2. Add hours for activities 8, 9, 10, 13 and 14 only for percent people-oriented effort	

Figure 48 : Weekly time log

Now think about your week ahead. First, plan in calls and purposeful meetings with key stakeholders. Set yourself some modest targets; say, one proactive conversation a day. You probably already have topics and new developments to discuss with them. We dealt with planning such meetings and calls under the How and When steps.

Practice: Starting earlier rather than later [Speculator]

Do it now. It is not safe to leave a generous feeling
to the cooling influences of the world.

-—Thomas Guthrie

Don't be tempted to leave this awkward 'communication thing' until last on your to-do list. This is a mistake. It is much better if you begin earlier. If you introduce yourself to people earlier and simply ask them questions, this is will generally be much more effective.

There are a number of reasons for this:

1.   The engagement pathway is progressive but iterative, not linear. Have you ever noticed how people often seem to need time to process information, and go back over ground already covered in previous conversations or meetings? They often need to go back and check each other's understanding. People like to consolidate their understanding as they proceed into an uncertain future. This is because human memory and the emotions that go with it are fragile and unreliable. People do not process experiences and their meaning in a machine-like way. Gaining understanding and mastery is not a one-off process. They need to be reminded of, and re-connected with, previously-covered topics; this allows them to develop their own sense of things.

2.   As you engage, you will learn new things, discover new stakeholders that you may not have yet considered.

3.   Generally speaking, people are much more favourably inclined towards a person who seeks them out first, than if they are told about a change from someone else after some lapse of time.

As emphasised in the first principle, going in with questions about them and their interests is one of the most powerful influencing strategies.

Consider this: if someone shows an interest in you first, aren't you more favourably inclined towards him or her? Try the opposite: approach a stranger and see how well

> **Exercise**: Call three people who are stakeholders, whom you haven't spoken with yet or haven't in a while, and ask them if you can meet to talk with them about something you are working on.

Why face-to-face still matters

> Let us make a special effort to stop communicating with each other, so we can have some conversation.
>
> **—Judith Martin**

There is a growing body of evidence[2] from the field of neuroscience to suggest that we are fooling ourselves into thinking that the written word is even half as effective as face-to-face in communicating a message.

It is fairly well established that most of the information we get in a face-to-face communication is not from the words themselves, but rather from body language, facial expression, and tone of voice. Body language is powerful.

At a very early age we learned to process body language, facial expressions, and tone of voice, even before we could speak. In contrast we had to spend years learning to read and write with any level of sophistication.

It seems that our brains expect these other, more significant, channels of information, and when they don't come, the brain becomes alarmed and distracted, thus impairing communication.

Part of the issue, researchers have discovered, is just how crucial is that immediate response. In still-face effect experiments with infants, for example, they learned that babies become immediately distressed when their mother maintains a "still face" that does not show any response or feedback with what the baby is doing. Whilst this is perhaps obvious, what's really interesting is when they experimented with video. In some of these variations on the still-face effect, mothers and babies were on closed-circuit monitors where they could

---

2   Abridged from a great post in Kathy Sierra's blog, *Creating Passionate Users*, which had, sadly, at the time of writing, lapsed.

each see each other in real-time, through a television monitor. The babies were much happier when their mother's face was responsive to their own, even less distressed than when the mother was right in front of the baby but maintaining a still face!

So, it was the responsiveness that mattered as well as the visual information. But just how quick does the feedback/response need to be? When they took the same experiment but introduced a short delay (no more than a few seconds), the babies became distressed again. Even a small degree of latency killed the feedback/interaction/responsiveness the baby's brain was expecting and needing.

Whilst we are now adults, and not babies, we still have the same basic neurochemistry, and no matter how much we practice communicating through text, the brain still finds it stressful. The only population whose lives have improved through the use of text over face-to-face are those with acute shyness. In the brains of the shy, a previously unknown face triggers a fear or anxiety response in their amygdala[3], which doesn't happen in text.

Video-conferencing is better than any other form of non face-to-face, because you get facial expressions, tone of voice, body language, AND real-time responsiveness. But there is still a very unsettling feature for the brain because there's really no way for BOTH speakers to make eye contact! If you look at the camera, then the other person sees you looking at them, but then your experience suffers. So you can either watch the person you're chatting with, which helps your experience but causes their's to suffer (since you won't be looking into the camera, so to *them* you'll be looking down), *or* you can look in the camera and improve their experience. But there's no way to have the camera right in your face, in a place where you can still look into the other person's eyes. Bottom line: You can see the camera or the person's eyes, but not both.

---

3   The part of the brain that has a primary function of processing memory and emotional responses.

And even with the benefits of adding video to your chat, there's still a lot the scientists don't know about other factors surrounding human communication that can't be captured electronically. Smell, for example, might be far more powerful than we might realise - even when below our conscious awareness.

So, what to do if you're like me, and you work remotely from team members for much of the time? Using video-conferencing, even over Skype or Google Hangout, is a big improvement. Often I ask my colleague to break off an audio-only phone call so that we can have a video chat. But ultimately there's no substitution for face-to-face. So anything you can do to try to interact with people face-to-face is very helpful. Even if it's just a once-a-year meeting, the very fact that you've had a chance to see and hear that person and experience them in front of you goes a long way towards helping you when you get back to your remote office and return to text.

Having face-to-face interaction is so crucial to the brain that, even if you can't do face-to-face with your team, you should try to make sure you have a healthy amount of live social interaction. So, join a local user group. Spend more time with friends. Attend conferences. And, most of all, consider reducing the amount of time you watch television. Part of it has to do with the way having the television tricks one part of your brain into thinking you're having a social interaction: all these people having conversations in your living room. But it fails to give the brain what it expects and needs from that interaction.

Finally, photos of your face help too, so if you dare (and circumstances permit), you should post a picture of your face somewhere and make sure people have it. Ask the person you're emailing if you can send a photo so they "know to whom they're talking" a little better, and ask if they'll do the same.

So why do most of us delude ourselves into thinking that, especially with text messaging, face-to-face is overrated? Most of us still attempt to influence through using words alone. Whilst deep relationships can develop and sustain through merely text correspondence, such instances are rare and demand significant commitment and discipline from both correspondents.

Practice: Respond fast or respond slow, but show it [Change Agent, Speculator]

So showing an immediate response in face-to-face contexts is important for a sense of security and meaningful rapport.

Immediacy of written response is different. Sometimes being too quick to respond in substance can create unnecessary work. So consider a quick courtesy holding reply ("I'll get back to you on that when I have given it more thought.").

You need to be seen to be responsive, but you also need to give yourself thinking time, and maybe a cooling-off period. A pause might reveal your idea as simply hare-brained or unintentionally offensive.

Technique: Taking the next step [Speculator]

One helpful approach from David Allen's work[4], is simply to ask yourself, *"What one thing can I do in the next 20 minutes to move me closer to realising my goal or outcome?"* Routinely asking this question helps you become a more positive, effective and pro-active leader.

For example, the answer to that question might be to pick up the phone and call that stakeholder, or to walk over to see them. Or it might be to prepare an interview plan for an important stakeholder meeting.

This can create a powerful momentum as you work through massive commitments than might otherwise cause you to procrastinate.

---

4   *Getting Things Done: How to Achieve Stress-Free Productivity* (Piatkus: 2002)

Practice: Getting out there [Speculator]

Ninety per cent of success is showing up.

—Woody Allen

Gardens are not made by singing, "Oh, how beautiful," and sitting in the shade.

—Rudyard Kipling

Maybe you are undermining your influence by an unhealthy over-reliance on email as your medium of influence.

A few years ago, the management fad was "Managing by Wandering Around" (MBWA). The emphasis is on wandering as an impromptu act, rather than a plan where people expect a visit from you at more systematic, pre-approved or scheduled times.

It deserved to be more than a fad, because, when done with the right motives and some emotional intelligence, it works. The tacit information you gain by wandering into a particular work area can be huge. You can perceive things that people who work there no longer notice. They could be "walking over the dead bodies."

Technique: Daily challenges [Speculator]

A knowledge worker is someone who gets to
decide what he does each morning.

—Thomas A. Stewart

Most of us find engagement difficult because it is strange. It is not one of our habits. It takes conscious effort to change this.

> **Exercise**: Set yourself a daily challenge of walking to a group, or to seeing someone face-to-face, or of calling someone rather than – or as well as - emailing. The target is to do this twice as much as you are doing at the moment, for the next four weeks. Then review your results.

Over time you will find yourself becoming more courageous. You "raise the bar" in terms of your engagement challenges. This could become one of your keystone habits.

Practice: Listening with humility [Leader]

If I only had a little humility, I'd be perfect.

—Ted Turner

Many struggle to "suffer fools gladly", as they see it. However, the very mindset of serving all the stakeholders helps bring us down to their level. If taking the other's perspective is a key skill for me in influencing people, it can be undermined if others perceive any arrogance in me.

What emerges is that humility in engaging with people becomes a paradox: it leads to powerful persuasion. Part of this is to exercise the other-perspective competence, considered earlier.

> Jim Collins, for the research project that was eventually published in his book, "Good to Great"[5], tells how he briefed his research team that he didn't want to hear about leadership, since he was somewhat unimpressed by much of the burgeoning literature on the subject. His team later came back to him and said, "It's Leadership, Jim, but not as we know it!" What they meant was that in their research into breakthrough organisations, leadership was a factor, but it was an odd sort of leadership, an iron resolve mixed with humility. He went on to call it Level 5 Leadership.

A fascinating treatise on Humility has been written by John Dickson[6], Senior Research Fellow of the Department of Ancient History at Macquarie University in Sydney, Australia. In it he writes, "We are more attracted to the great who are humble than to the great who know it and want everyone else to know it as well."[7]

---

5   *Good to Great: Why some companies make the leap … and others don't*, Random House Business, 2001).
6   *Humilitas*, (Zondervan, 2011)
7   Ibid. p.69.

> You see, when there is danger, a good leader takes the front line. But
> when there is celebration, a good leader stays in the back room. If
> you want the cooperation of human beings around you, make them
> feel that they are important. And you do that by being humble.

—Nelson Mandela

Dickson's argument is that humility not only leads to a higher order of leadership, as Jim Collins discovered, but that:

1. It is just common sense: "What we can know and do is far exceeded by what we do not know and cannot do. Expertise in one area counts for very little in other areas."

2. Humility is generative. It generates new knowledge. He cites a long list of scientists and researchers. "The humble place is the generative place, the place of flourishing."

3. Humility is persuasive. Aristotle wrote the best textbook on persuasion for 2000 years in 'On Rhetoric'. He argued there must be ethos - the character of the persuader - and the ethos is the most important part of the argument.

4. Humility is inspiring. See the Mandela quote above. Where otherwise able leaders have stumbled, it is where they have lacked humility. (He gives the example of Steve Jobs, the iPhone 4 and 'antennagate', with Jobs' apparent inability to admit fault.)

> When we take a lower position it is so powerful from
> a service provider's position. Show people that you
> are willing to do whatever they ask you to do.

—Patrick Lencioni

In summary, then, genuine humility before stakeholders is likely to be powerfully persuasive, allowing you to truly listen, and to influence far beyond what the arrogant are able to achieve. I believe many of us know this intuitively.

Technique: Active listening [Change Agent]

Active listening is a technique that emphasises the listener's need to feedback what they have heard. This begins to overcome a common weakness in conversations where the listener is "waiting to be heard" rather than really listening. The technique of Active Listening[8] is a process of five conscious steps. They include:

1. **Observing**. Non-evaluative attention to verbal and non-verbal communication.

2. **Reflecting back**. Rephrasing what they have said in your own words, so improving clarity and signaling that you are really listening.

3. **Summarising**. Often helpful to the other person in articulating what they might have been trying to say in a few words.

4. **Reflecting feelings**. Honouring the emotional intent, and so signaling that we not only understand the content, but empathises with the feelings conveyed. This is very powerful in active listening, often convincing the other person that they have been 'really' understood.

5. **Interpreting**. Sometimes helpful, in making connections with conclusions or implications that may have been unsaid. But be careful not to distort what the listener actually meant.

    Exercise: Try this active listening technique as an experiment. It is one of several such, which need to be experienced rather than merely understood.

    Plan a meeting using these five phases/steps.

---

8   See J. Dan Rothwell, *In the Company of Others: An introduction to communication*, (Oxford University Press: 2009).

At the end of the meeting, consider the outcome and richness of the consequent conversations. Did the other parties feel more appreciated and open up more? Were there surprising disclosures? Were there surprising solutions that emerged?

Practice: Making purposeful conversations [Change Agent]

> Conversation doesn't just reshuffle the cards:
> it creates new cards
>
> **—Theodore Zeldin**

Oxford Professor Theodore Zeldin[9] similarly values the richness of conversations where there is a greater weight placed on the act of purposeful listening. Such conversations can have surprisingly profound outcomes.

> A good conversation is neither aimless nor empty.
>
> **—Mortimer J. Adler**

By now, you might be reappraising the value of the humble conversation. People practiced in intentional conversations gain much, for themselves and for the change they are trying to lead.

> We risk impoverishing ourselves if we ignore the personal.
>
> **—David Gurteen**

Consider making the conversation a deliberate part of your execution. Conversations, and your ability to make them more useful, will improve in potency as you practice them.

> I contend that conversations are the stem cells of learning.
>
> **—Jay Cross**

---

9   *Conversation: How Talk can Change our Lives* (Hidden Spring, 2000).

Conversations can range along a spectrum from one extreme where we know the outcome we want to achieve from the conversation, to one which is much more unknown[10]. Usually people have more difficulty with beginning the latter kind of conversations. The issues that inhibit us are often fear of the unknown, fear of rejection and not knowing how to begin.

Most of us who conduct job interviews have been taught to prepare open questions, not closed questions: i.e. ones that can be answered with a mere "Yes" or "No". This is a conversational strategy that deserves more use.

> **Exercise**: Create some conversation opening questions.
> Here is one example: "What is the one thing you would
> like to change about your job?"
>
> Create five more. Use them in the next few conversations
> you have. Reflect on how these conversations went as a
> consequence.

---

10   See the following practice: "Vary engagement modes appropriately."

Practice: Varying engagement modes appropriately [Leader]

I have emphasised the great potency and value of conversations. Conversations have great range in all kinds of situations. As this diagram shows:

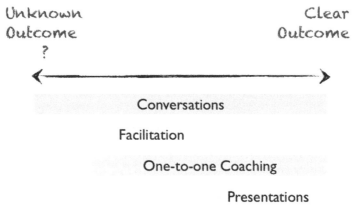

Figure 49 : Engagement Modes

Conversations can be exploratory with a stakeholder, where you are uncertain what the result might be, as well as a means of moving a stakeholder from one position to another.

At the individual level, there are other modes, where you engage by being physically present. Facilitation is where you guard the process of a group discussion as a neutral, or you might bring someone in so that you too can fully participate with everyone else.

One-to-one coaching becomes relevant particularly in supporting an individual's transition, where learning new skills and behaviours is critical to the change being successful. However, coaching too can bring to the surface some surprises.

Finally, there is the presentation, which takes on a level of formality. A good presentation aims for a particular result. It is not usually the place for dialogue, but a good presenter needs to prepare for interruptions; even heckling on some occasions!

It is not the purpose of this book to go deep into the art and science of each of these, but there are some further references at the back. However, check your Communications Plan.

- Does it have sufficient variety in its engagement modes?

- Is each mode used appropriately?

Practice: Talking about life beyond delivery [Leader]

When I was a teenager I took up Karate. In terms of self-esteem, self-protection and street-credibility, it had an effect on me: I didn't see the school bully for dust! One of the sensational things about Karate for me at the time was how experts were able to chop, punch or kick through wood or concrete with their bare hands or feet. The trick, I was told, was to focus the strike beyond the thing you were trying to break and so carry the blow through.

A crucial aspect to achieving high performance through communications is rather similar: you must break out of the project life cycle, the plan to mere delivery. As the karate black belt aims for a point beyond the block of concrete, you must communicate beyond your delivery. That is to say, talk about life afterwards.

Your clients are often not the least bit interested in what you deliver. Rather they are more concerned about how they will use the stuff you give them, how it will change their working patterns, how it might make their lives better or worse.

Even during the life cycle, you will gain much more engagement with your clients if you discuss what you do in terms of how it will affect them beyond delivery of the new thing. So communicate with punch, aiming for a point beyond delivery. [But try not to yell when you do it... You'll find the analogy breaks down here...]

What will help you to do this is if you have a written vision or a 'user story' from the point of view of the person with whom you are talking. Recall the Value Ladder to help you structure these conversations.

In her book *Changing Conversations*[11], Patricia Shaw shows that sincere engagement with people through conversations often in and of itself changes people's positions, usually positively, and results in some very creative contributions from stakeholders, sometimes stakeholders who have previously offered nothing but resistance.

Practice: Engaging with difficult people [Leader]

Be kind, for everyone you meet is fighting a hard battle.

—Plato

Leaders always move towards a problem.

—Bill Hybels

It seems we are bound to encounter people we come to regard as difficult, wherever we work. There can be any number of reasons why someone appears difficult to do business with. It is a fact of life. So how do we engage them?

There is no 'silver bullet' for such situations. But here is one influencing strategy. It is mostly a synthesis of one of Stephen Covey's *7 Habits of Highly Effective People*[12] along with elements from *Getting to Yes*[13], the best-selling work on negotiation by Roger Fisher et al. There are other strategies. This one is not guaranteed to work every time with everybody but, by following it, you will be better prepared, and get more successful outcomes over a number of such 'confrontations' than you would do otherwise.

---

11   *Changing Conversations in Organizations: A Complexity Approach to Change* (Routledge, 2002).
12   *The 7 Habits of Highly Effective People* (Simon & Schuster: 1999).
13   *Getting to Yes: Negotiating an Agreement without Giving In* (Random House: 1997).

1. **Be clear on your BATNA** ('Best Alternative to a Negotiated Agreement'). Part of being understood by the other party is to have clarity in your own mind what are the non-negotiable aspects of your own position. You need to be clear in your own mind about what your fall-back position will be if you can't get agreement - your BATNA.

    Fisher et al. argue that going into tough negotiations without a BATNA immediately puts you into a position of weakness. You must have an alternative available, even if you never use it.

    Your BATNA could be, among other things:

    » Some strong escalation to more senior, more powerful people.

    » Some radical re-scoping to exclude the need for cooperation from this stakeholder (usually risky).

    » Even in the most extreme cases conceding that your initiative or project should be stopped altogether.

    These are only generic options. In specific cases you may be able to identify others and you strengthen you position if you can identify more.

    Remember that this is the best alternative, and not a spurious alternative: to offer a false BATNA would be a bluff, pretentious brinkmanship ... and you risk the other party calling your bluff!

2. **Seek first to understand** (our first Principle). Earn the right to be heard by them by listening to them first. Listen to their heart as well as their head, the emotional 'music'. In doing this you are giving them the dignity of being treated like a human being and not just a block or an obstacle, or someone who has to be humoured or to whom you need to pander.

In hostile situations, where we consider going into some conflict, as humans it is natural for us all to de-humanise the enemy. You need to be aware of this tendency in yourself and resist it. Difficult people are not always the enemy, and to make them so can worsen matters.

3.   **Reflect back that you understand them**. Re-playing, as accurately as you can their position, showing that you can empathise with their pain or sense of threat as well as their rational argument, is usually far more effective that the "Yes, but" sort of response we all usually fall into. This often takes the sting immediately out of the dialogue. It may not be vocalised, but the other party is thinking, "Ah! So you do understand where I'm coming from!" This relates to one of the steps in Active Listening (see above).

4.   **Then be understood**. "Thank you for helping me to understand where you are coming from. So allow me to make my position

Figure 50 : The difficult stakeholder strategy

clear and I think we might find we are not so far apart." This flags that you are not about to be a doormat and be walked all over. You have a position and you need to be heard. Make that clear.

Notice also there was no "but" in that response. Your aim is to get alongside the other party and look at the difficulty together.

5. **Seek 'Win-win' or 'No deal'.** You should know their 'WIIFM' ('what's in it for me?'). What benefits could there be in your change for that stakeholder. What are the 'wins' for them? Reference your Benefits Distribution Matrix, if you have developed one. This is a deeper and more personal level of stakeholder analysis that is particularly warranted for the difficult individual. Often reviewing the scope of the change together with the stakeholder gives you both a chance to optimise the benefits and reduce the perceived dis-benefits for them. However, remember that a benefit for you might well be a dis-benefit to the other party and vice versa.

   One the keys to agile negotiation is to discover other unmet wants or needs of the other party that you might be able to help satisfy or provide if they are prepared to meet your needs.

6. **Make the 'Ask'.** Often engagement fails because we don't summon up the courage to make the ultimate request (the 'Ask') of the other party when we have the opportunity. I find sales people understand this; they call it 'closing.' Often we can 'make the Ask' of the other party in a way that acknowledges that it would be costly for them in some way, but thereby implying that they would be courageous or magnanimous to do it. Simply making the request in that way can seem very affirming to the other party.

7. **Reflect back the consequences**, if necessary, **of their action or inaction.** Explain what will happen if they do not work on this initiative with you, or if they delay making the decision. Spell out the increased costs, the reduced benefits, and how this will play out... all as a consequence of their (in) action or stance.

   Obviously, you will need to prepare this argument in advance, in case you need it. It may call for you to secure approval in principle from their more senior managers first for their cooperation in achieving your objectives.

This can be particularly powerful and clarifying where the stakeholder does not yet appreciate the unintended consequences of their position. You may even need to go a step further by making it clear that their actions and the consequences will be visible to others, possibly to those to whom they are accountable. Ask, "How would they feel about that?"

This is can be an important issue with some decision-makers who are prone to hesitate or procrastinate in giving you approval to proceed. Very rarely do decision-makers appreciate the full cost of delaying their decision. It's your responsibility to make that clear to them as best you can to them. ("Well, if I can't get your agreement today, we miss an opportunity to move and this will set back the whole schedule six weeks, incurring $xxx additional cost.")

It's remarkable how frequently people reassess their position when confronted, albeit sensitively but assertively, with such potential consequences.

> We all forgive ourselves too easily. We all find it quite easy to live with guilt. Even a high level of guilt doesn't always change people. However, embarrassment, even in small doses, can be far more effective.

—David Maister[14]

Not enough is discussed in business literature about the need for plain courage. To some extent it 'costs' you, and it 'costs' the stakeholder. Let the challenge of meeting with this stakeholder in this way and of wrestling with them become part of your mutual 'story' that can be shared with them and others at the right moments.

Disclaimer: I am not presenting this approach in any way as a foolproof strategy for dealing with all difficult people. There is no such thing. When dealing with some people, you are always taking a considered risk, whatever strategy you use. You use this at your own risk.

14   From *Strategy and the Fat Smoker: Doing what's obvious but not easy* (The Spangle Press: 2008).

Practice: Aiming to delight your customer [Marketer]

You gotta serve somebody.

—Bob Dylan

The purpose of business is to create and keep a customer.

—Peter F. Drucker

The focus for high performance in business is right here in actively engaging people. With the right mindset and having worked through the other steps to get this far, it is good to remind yourself that your aim is to delight your customer. This can mean delivering beyond expectations set, or just consistently delivering on your promises in a pleasant, supportive manner.

However, you might point me to the fact that not all your stakeholders are customers. That is very true and very pertinent. And trying to please everybody is the route to failure, not high performance. For example, in the charity sector, volunteers in the organisation often behave as if they are the shareholders; always going with them may get you nowhere.

So, be clear who your customer really is, and then go all out to delight them.

Practice: Improvising [Speculator]

Compared to the length of the chapter on the How Step in this book you could be forgiven for thinking that I give more weight to analysis than I do to execution. I do not. The reason that this chapter is shorter is because a common experience is, once immersed in execution, that

the very experience of engagement

becomes the best teacher of all

Improvisation is one skill that is best developed in practice. It is by definition something that defies prescription. It requires a degree of spontaneous creativity and risk-taking. It employs the kind of rapport we discussed earlier.

We have all had sales experiences where the seller is clearly and mechanistically following some sort of script. This very rarely impresses anyone. The ability to improvise, to listen and respond, to develop rapport with the other person, to "roll with the punches" and adjust to the person in front of you is an important ability. Out of it comes a real connection. This picks up the theme earlier in the discussion on why 'Ambiverts' tend to be more influential.

In business we have the institution of so-called 'beauty parades': potential suppliers being asked to give a presentation of their proposals. Everyone I've talked with about this practice agrees it is a very artificial, awkward process. Many progressive businesses have abandoned it in favour of two-way pre-sales conversations, and they seem to get better outcomes as a result. Why do these beauty parades still persist? It seems it is the influence of the gatekeepers again.

> Once I found myself as the lead presenter in an important pitch for business from a prospective client, a global telecoms business. I had my presentation script and began to take the interviewing panel through it. Fairly early into this, one of the clients interrupted, clearly the leader, who corrected me on one of our key assumptions.
>
> I responded by taking a moment and then confessing that what we had prepared was probably quite inappropriate. It was a huge risk.

We spent the rest of the 'pitch' in an exploratory conversation with the panel.

We won the business.

Living the principles in the Engage Step

Seek first to understand and then be understood: The Engage Step may be the first time you speak with some people. Engagement's strongest opener in any conversation is always something like, "What do you feel about this?" Invariably people open up and tell you.

Effective change is always led: Crossing the room to talk to someone is quintessentially a leadership behaviour. A leader, as we saw in the Bennis table, works through relating to people. Courageous leadership is called for when engaging apparently difficult stakeholders.

Habits are the inhibitors and the goal of change: The allied habits of leaning into relationships and leaning to action are critical, and they need to be exhibited in one very important stakeholder: you. Practice this step until these become your habits. It can feel tough at first; you are breaking the mould of traditional management behaviour. Living this principle will get easier with practice. Remember the engagement bicycle. You may wobble a bit at first, but you get more capable with practice.

Recognise and minimise the pain of change: Engaging, particularly face-to-face, helps you see pain as much as hear complaints from people. It creates opportunities sometimes to act in a way that can surprise them by minimising their pain.

High performance comes through people and action: In addition to the comments in the discussion above on habits, work spent in engagement begins to scale the change, to align people around you so that they become champions for it too.

Integrity is powerfully persuasive: One indispensable way of showing your stakeholders you are genuine is to meet with them, listen, and show you are listening.

Feelings trump reason, and meaning trumps authority: We have already shown that feelings are best expressed face-to-face. Giving your stakeholders the gift of time also demonstrates that this change is important enough for you to do this. Most people will give you a hearing, and will listen for meaning. This is your chance to explain why this is worth their attention and effort.

When to take this Step

- You should *always* be practicing this Step, even if you are doing so cautiously.

Engage Step - Summary

- Prioritise your diary to spend more time with people, preferably face-to-face where possible

- Set about stakeholder engagement as one of the first things you do and do it continuously, regularly throughout the change

- Of all the chapters on the practice of engagement in this book, this Step is the most important one. Action trumps everything

- Check you are not procrastinating on the uncomfortable business of contacting sometimes difficult, sometimes unpleasant, people, or fearing rejection

- Face-to-face is the most powerful mode of engagement. Use it

- Engagement through conversations is ubiquitous, but consider other modes of engagement

- Talk about how their life might be different beyond delivery. This can be a very positive and powerful way of changing the conversation

- Make sure people see that you are responding to their concerns and requirements. Note: this is responding to, not necessarily complying with, what they want

- With difficult stakeholders 'seek win-win or no deal'; and make sure you have a BATNA. If necessary, point out the consequences of their non-cooperation

- Be clear who your customer is, and aim to delight them.

- Dare to improvise and learn as you engage.

Engage Step Practices

- Prioritising your time

- Start earlier rather than later

- Respond fast or respond slow, but show it

- Getting out there

- Listening with humility

- Purposeful conversations

- Varying engagement modes appropriately

- Talking about life beyond delivery

- Engaging with difficult people

- Aiming to delight your customer

- Improvising

Engage Step Techniques

- The Next Step

- Daily challenges

- Active listening.

CHAPTER 13

The Adapt Step: Measure, adapt, improve

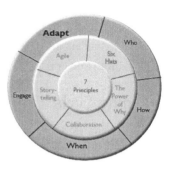

You shall know the truth, and the truth shall set you free.

—Jesus of Nazareth

Confront the brutal reality.

Jim Collins and Jerry Porras[1]

Go to bed smarter than when you woke up.

Charlie Munger

R eality is your friend. Knowing how well or badly you are achieving your engagement gives you vital evidence and motivation to go on, to adjust or to re-think your approach. The key is to know when, where and how to adapt.

---

1   *Built to Last: Successful Habits of Visionary Companies*, (Random House Business, 2005).

A serious weakness in otherwise-good stakeholder engagement is not tracking how you are doing. You can easily deceive yourself that you are doing really well, that your change is well regarded, when the real perceptions held by your stakeholders are quite different. This can be a kind of denial: you might prefer not to find out. You need mechanisms to check.

Deming Cycle

W. E. Deming, the legendary quality guru who took quality practices to post-War Japan and helped revolutionise their manufacturing sector, developed this cycle which he illustrated was the key to continuous improvement:

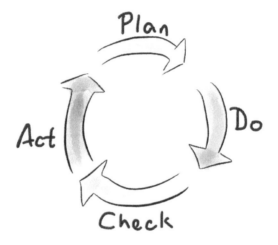

Figure 51 : The Deming Cycle

The Deming Cycle also holds the key to high performance people engagement. It focuses on evidence. So, in your context, what evidence do you have of engagement and alignment with your work? How can you prove it? This begins to build true rigour and effectiveness into your work. It tells the lie to the sceptics around you who maintain that all this engagement stuff is just "wishy-washy" nonsense.

Much of the engagement pathway has been devoted to the first phase in Deming's cycle: **Plan**. It was difficult to avoid exploring plan in so much detail. But you need to stand back now and see the whole pathway in perspective.

The next phase in the cycle is **Do**. This maps nicely onto our Engage Step.

This Adapt Step is very much about how you will work through the other two phases of Deming's cycle: **Check** and **Act**.

Check is at its most rigorous when you have something to check against. For example, your stakeholder target positions, the emotional state you need a stakeholder to have moved to, and so on. Further rigour is provided by consequential measures of true engagement, such as benefit realisation plans and performance targets.

Act includes the corrective adjustments you are prompted to make from that evidence. Perhaps feedback from one group of stakeholders is worryingly negative. The corrective action might be to change your strategy, or it might be suggested from the feedback itself, pointing to some omission on your part.

Once the correction is made, then appropriately readjust your analysis and strategy (less likely) or plan and execution (usually more likely). Based on the evidence you might even be prompted to revisit your overall perspective on stakeholder engagement, and re-balance your working week accordingly.

On the more positive side, the Check phase can uncover success stories, early victories, and unexpected champions, of which you might have been otherwise unaware until much later. In these happy situations the Act phase is simply mobilising or capitalising on all of this good news.

Interestingly this cycle has been central to much of Agile development thinking. The effort is more focused on generating and testing the *empirical* evidence of quality, rather than on written specifications.

Practice: Seek independent review
[Marketer, Accountant]

If possible, get independent reviewers, people outside of your change team. Otherwise you risk people telling you what they think you want to hear, in order to be nice to you, perhaps, or to avoid a difficult conversation. Sometimes they tell you what you want to hear in order to hide their own confusion and perceived incompetence.

Since you may have become the message and the change (as with the President Jimmy Carter illustration earlier) to many of your stakeholders, it is often helpful to get somebody impartial, who isn't seen as aligned to your agenda to ask the review questions.

On larger change programmes with a Programme Office, there could well be appropriate specialist skills in communication and engagement. If not, then perhaps there is a corporate PR or communications office whom you could call on to review your engagement.

Technique: The Net Promoter Score [Accountant]
What's measured improves.

Peter F. Drucker

'Customer satisfaction' is a relevant concept here. In recent years the Reicheld scale has become widely adopted as people have come to appreciate its power.

Below is the Reicheld scale (more commonly known as 'the Net Promoter Score') developed by Fred Reicheld, who spent twenty-five years researching customer satisfaction and how to measure it. After much experimentation, he found the question that worked the best was as follows, measured on an eleven-point scale (0 to 10):

"How likely is it that you will recommend this firm or service or product to a colleague or friend?"

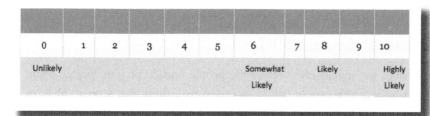

Figure 52 : Net Promoter Scale

He classed people who responded into three groups, depending on their scoring:

0 - 6	Detractors
7, 8	Passively satisfied
9, 10	Promoters

Overall he measured client delight using this formula:

%Promoters - %Detractors = %Net Promoters

Whilst it has its limitations, currently this measure is generally considered the best available, as well as being practical and intuitive.

Try it – with appropriate changes to the question wording – on your change initiative and see what effect it has. You might find that merely conducting the survey has a positive effect on some stakeholders' view of you and your change. However, it will help you and your team focus more on stakeholder satisfaction.

If you have a project management office or a centre of excellence function in your organisation, it may have skills within it to help you conduct such a survey[2].

Technique: Daily stand-up [Leader, Accountant]

We are continually faced by great opportunities brilliantly disguised as insoluble problems.

—Lee Iococca

This is a technique used in Scrum, an Agile development method, and a variant of it in DSDM. It has become the mainstay of the Agile iterative cycle. As its name implies, it is a daily meeting, usually at the beginning of the working day, when the team gathers to consider three questions to which every team member answers in turn:

1. What have we/I achieved since yesterday?

2. What are we/I going to do today?

3. What impediments/hindrances am I encountering?

---

2   The Review and Revise Practice in the How Step is likely to be relevant here.

Again as the name implies, everyone stands, which makes for short and rapid meetings.

This injects a daily Review Step where you can take corrective actions immediately. Monitoring and adaptation are thus built into the team's working day.

Stephen Denning writes:

> The shift in language from "What are the problems?" to "What are the impediments?' is significant. "Problems" may arise from unhappiness for any number of reasons. "Impediments" relate to goals. "What is preventing us from delighting clients?" An airing of impediments focuses the discussion on what is getting in the way of reaching the common goal.[3]

This technique is particularly helpful where the team has to refrain from documented stakeholder profiles, perhaps for reasons of confidentiality or sensitivity. In these cases, mobilising the team's intelligence on overt and tacit stakeholder characteristics in daily stand-ups becomes brisk, professional and current.

Living the principles in the Adapt Step

Seek first to understand, and then be understood: This Step checks that you and your team have been understood as intended. It is also likely to reveal a fresh understanding of people that will help you in later iterations of engagement.

Effective change is always led: This Chapter began with a quote from "Built to Last", about confronting the brutal reality. Reality can be brutal and this is where change is led. Leaders do confront reality when others would rather live in denial or habit.

Habits are the inhibitors and the goal: The Adapt Step, from the empirical evidence of feedback and observed behaviour, helps you track how habits are really changing. Habits become a key performance indicator of engagement.

---

3   Denning, *The Leader's Guide to Radical Management,* op. cit. p. 179.

Recognise and minimise the pain of change: The Adapt Step helps you discover pain where before it might have not been recognised. Review helps you immediately take action and adapt, to adjust your course and correct to minimise pain. This in turn can be a powerful influencing response, where those in pain see you responding to relieve it.

High performance comes through people and action: This Step is the essence of living this principle. Reviewing by asking people is leaning towards them, and adapting and re-shaping as a result of this empirical evidence is action-oriented.

Integrity is powerfully persuasive: What could be more honest than a genuine search for the answer to, "How is it going, *really*?" Gaining stakeholder opinions and acting on them demonstrates your genuine, caring responsiveness.

Feelings trump reason and meaning trumps authority: Discovering the clarity people really have about the reason for your change is vital. One time I tested how well the vision in a third sector organisation had been explained by asking random volunteers, "What is your vision?" The result was that about three out of five could recite the short vision verbatim, which I believe was pretty good. But also testing the emotional temperature is important. Leaders need to stay connected with the current mood and morale of the people they seek to lead.

When to take this Step

- At the end of every phase of your engagement as laid out in your strategy and plan.

- If some threat materialises from among your stakeholders, such as an unexpected strong opposition to what you are trying to do.

- If you are unsure at any point about a potential stakeholder reaction and want to gauge their response indirectly.

Adapt Step Summary

- Reality is your friend. So measure it

- It's too easy to be fooled that engagement is going well; people can give the wrong impression, tell you what they think you want to hear, hide their own confusion and perceived incompetence

- An adapted Net Promoter Score or Reicheld Scale is something you should consider using

- Asking people for their sense of engagement is in itself engaging

- Independent review can be more objective.

Adapt Step Practice

- The practice in this step is to seek independent review.

Adapt Step Techniques

- The Net Promoter Score

- The Daily Stand-Up.

Final words

Of course, in reality there are no sequential steps in stakeholder engagement. The steps explained in this book can be done all at the same time - and often are. Life is simply not that neat and tidy. It can seem very chaotic in the communications you try to plan and the relationships you try to build. You are likely to experience stakeholder engagement as anything but linear. At best it is iterative, similar to agile development cycles.

The reason I have set out the steps in this way is because:

the map is not the territory

This saying is true for all management frameworks and methods. A map is not an exact representation of the territory you cross; it never can be. But it can orient you and it can help you make important decisions on your way.

Treat these five steps as building a pathway of engagement. Your experience will be different in detail, but the steps will help you make better, more informed decisions. Tending to follow the steps in sequence will give you better results than if you try to do everything at once. Just don't be too anxious if real life gets in the way and you have to jump around the steps somewhat.

Finally if this book was of help to you, please do let me know. If you think it can be improved at all, also let me know. Even let me have your Reicheld scale score for this book (Adapt Step). Your feedback is most welcome, crucial, in fact.

Thank you and I wish you every success with leading your stakeholders.

Patrick Mayfield

@PatrickMayfield

Appendix:
The Portfolio
Perspective

A portfolio is the totality of all projects and programmes, and related activities for an organisation or part of an organisation. More organisations are implementing the portfolio level of governance finding, among other benefits, that it provides a vital strategic link with the 'change agenda', helps reduce the waste of work that is irrelevant to strategy, and provides confidence to senior management about their capital investment in change[1].

At the portfolio level there exists a paradox: the portfolio view is strategic, the big picture of all the change activities going on in an organisation, but at the same time the analysis of that portfolio needs to be quite granular or detailed. More often than not, it is the lack of people availability or cooperation that limits the speed of overall change through a portfolio; people are usually the most constraining 'resource'. So these scarce, constraining resources are typically stakeholders as groups of people, or even sometimes an individual with a unique skill, ability or authority.

For example, say the strategic intent of an organisation is to move its retail online. The speed of doing this might be limited by the scarce technical skills in e-commerce. So the whole portfolio awaits the availability of these few web 'techies' to tackle the next project or programme in the backlog of the portfolio. So the portfolio office might optimise the phasing of much of the portfolio largely around the availability of these few people. If we want more speed through the backlog of programmes and projects, one solution is to increase the number of people with those skills - either by recruiting more of these specialists or outsourcing more of this kind of work to specialist suppliers.

---

1   There are a number of helpful references to portfolio management. In recent years one of the best is Jenner and Kilford's *Management of Portfolios* (TSO: 2011).

The problem becomes more subtle when the critical resource availability switches from those with scarce development skills, to those in operational business units.

Again, using our example, we could find that the limiting resource on parts of the portfolio is not among the developers but is a business unit that is struggling to service the retail work flow through shops and cannot find time to release key staff to qualify the work of the web publishers. This could be a chronic problem for this business unit, which by habit prioritises old model work requirements over the new web-retailing development work. It could be an acute seasonal problem, where these people are flat-out in the run-up to Christmas, but have spare time earlier on in the calendar year to work with the developers.

There is a third case where the portfolio perspective can see certain constraints causing problems for a particular business unit: where two otherwise-independent initiatives in the portfolio demand transitions on the same business unit *at the same time*. So the programme for web retailing needs this business unit to work on commissioning the web-purchases system in February to March, say, but at the same time a new budgeting roll-out also requires their time for training on new budget codes. This could lead to the business unit being overloaded. Only from looking at the demands on this stakeholder from the portfolio perspective can we gauge their true change readiness overall.

So then, if you work in an organisation with portfolio management, then the portfolio perspective will provide you with a valuable global perspective. Further, expect the portfolio management, if you have it, to become a key stakeholder of your own change from time to time.

Thanks to...

And Thanks To...

One of the emergent themes in this book is collaboration and its genesis itself is testimony to the power of collaboration. In truth, the contributions of others made it far better than if I had just forged ahead on my own.

I'm grateful to Keith Williams, Steve Jenner, David King and Mark Withers, all of whom have been profoundly formative in shaping my thinking in this area. I'm not only grateful for the all-too rare opportunities of working with each of them, but also for the valuable insights they gave me in the course of writing this.

Rick Price has always been a first class non-executive director to me, and helped with key steers and encouragement in the early course course of drafting this. Graham Devine, Matt Delany, Nathalie Collister and Graham Shreeve each contributed key insights that significantly improved and added to what I would have published otherwise. Among my clients Bryan Dowling of Butterfield Bank, Bruce Tanner of the Foreign & Commonwealth Office, and Jemima Alder of Elsevier gave of their valuable time. Richard Smith, Tony Mann and David Elverson responded kindly from related professional fields with valuable observations. Arnav Banerjee of Transport for London gave me encouraging and valuable input. Thanks also to Mary Henson, Victor Page and Jules Godwin of the DSDM Consortium for their fast and positive feedback; very much in keeping with the DSDM philosophy! Mike Acaster took time out during his transition to a new role in AXELOS to give me some encouraging feedback.

James Davies of APM Group has been supportive throughout, managing to fit in his wedding around my book project. I'm particularly grateful to Graham Williams for giving up much of his time in contributing a different perspective on the structuring of early drafts, and for making good my lack of strength in certain areas. Lenny Deschamps was a warmly supportive of the book from the start. Louise Esplin and Gail Yates were very helpful in certain design issues. Mila Perry came up with the winning design for this book; thanks to her for her creativity and patience with me. Elaine Taylor for her time and technical expertise.

Of course, my colleagues at pearcemayfield have all been very supportive: Adrian Boorman, Richard Rose, Anne Bellingan and John Edmonds. lubaid Khan worked his brilliance in setting up ppethebook.com. I hope this final product is some return for the personal support you each have given me. I'm always grateful for working with such a great team. Such teams definitely trump individuals.

Finally, thanks to all my clients, delegates on change management courses and on *Engaging Your Project Stakeholders* workshops. You have sharpened up my thinking and enriched my bank of stories immeasurably. You are testimony to how the Engage Step *is* the most important step, despite what the structured, theoretical types say.

Further Resources

I have set up a site to go with this book that will help you with further resources and updates. You will find it at www.ppethebook.com .

Works referenced in this book are as follows:

References

Allen, David, Getting Things Done: How to Achieve Stress-Free Productivity (Piatkus: 2002)

Association for Project Management, APM Body of Knowledge (6th Edition, 2012)

- APM Competence Framework (2008)

Bandler, R., Grinder, J. Frogs into Princes: Neuro Linguistic Programming. (Real People Press, 1979).

Beckhard, R F and Harris, R T, Organizational Transitions: Managing Complex Change, (Addison-Wesley, 1987).

Benjamin & Levinson citation. Benjamin, R. I. and Levinson, E. (1993). "A Framework for Managing IT-Enabled Change." Sloan Management Review, Summer: 23-3

Bennis, Warren, Authentic Leadership: Rediscovering the Secrets to Creating Lasting Value (Jossey-Bass, 1994).

Cameron, Esther, and Green, Mike, Making Sense of Change Management: A Complete Guide to the Models Tools and Techniques of Organizational Change (3rd Edition) (Kogan Page: 2012)

Collins, Jim & Porras, Jerry, Built to Last: Successful Habits of Visionary Companies (Random House: 2005)

Collins, Jim, Good to Great: Why some companies make the leap ... and others don't, (Random House Business: 2001).

Covey, Stephen R. Principle-Centred Leadership (Simon & Schuster: 1999)
-   The 7 Habits of Highly Effective People (Simon & Schuster: 2004)

Crowe, Andy, Alpha Project Managers: What the Top 2 Per Cent Know That Everyone Else Does Not (Velociteach Press, 2006).

Denning, Stephen, The Leader's Guide to Storytelling: Mastering the art and discipline of business narrative (Jossey-Bass, 2005).
-   The Leader's Guide to Radical Management: Re-inventing the Workplace for the 21st Century (Jossey Bass: 2010)

Decker, Bert, You've Got to be Believed to be Heard: The Complete Book of Speaking in Business and in Life (St Martins Press: 2008)

De Bono, Edward, Six Thinking Hats (Penguin, 2009).

DeMarco, Tom, & Lister, Tim, Peopleware: Productive Projects and Teams 2nd Edition (Dorset House Publishing: 1999)

Duarte, Nancy, Slide:ology: The Art and Science of Creating Great Presentations: The Art and Science of Presentation Design (O'Reilly Media: 2008)

Duhigg, Charles, The Power of Habit: Why We Do What We Do, and How to Change, (Random House Books, 2013).

Egan, Gerard, Working the Shadow Side: A Guide to Positive Behind-the-Scenes Management (Jossey-Bass, 1994)

Fisher, Roger, et al. Getting to Yes: Negotiating an Agreement without Giving In (Random House: 1997)

Frankl, Viktor, Man's Search for Meaning: The Classic Tribute to Hope from the Holocaust (Rider: 2004)

Gardner, Howard E., & Laskin, Emma, Leading Minds: An Anatomy of Leadership (Basic Books; Reprint edition, 2011)

Goleman, Daniel, Working with Emotional Intelligence (Bloomsbury, 1999).

Hall, Doug, Jump Start Your Business Brain: Six Scientific Laws for Thinking Smarter and More Creatively About Business Growth (Brain Brew Books, 2001)

- Meaningful Marketing (Brain Brew Books, 2003)

- Jump Start Your Marketing Brain (Brain Brew Books, 2007)

Heath, Chip and Dan Heath, Made to Stick: why some ideas take hold and others come unstuck (Arrow: 2008)

- Switch: How to change things when change is hard (Random House Business: 2011)

Jenner, Stephen, Managing Benefits: Optimizing the Return from Investments (Stationery Office, 2012).

Jenner, Stephen, and Kilford, Craig, Management of Portfolios (Cabinet Office, TSO: 2011)

Kahan, Seth, Getting Change Right: How Leaders Transform Organizations from the Inside Out (Jossey-Bass: 2010)

Kay, John, Obliquity: Why Goals are Best Achieved Indirectly (Profile: 2011)

Kahneman, Daniel, Thinking, Fast and Slow (Penguin, 2012)

Kotter, John P., Leading Change (Harvard Business School Press: 1996)

- The Heart of Change: Real-Life Stories of How People Change their Organizations (Harvard Business Press: 2002)

Kubler-Ross, Elisabeth, On Grief and Grieving: Finding the Meaning of Grief Through the Five Stages of Loss (Simon & Schuster: 2005)

Lewin, Kurt, Resolving Social Conflicts / Field Theory in Social Science (American Psychological Association: 1997)

Managing Successful Programmes (Cabinet Office, TSO: 2011)

Managing Successful Projects using PRINCE2 (Cabinet Office, TSO: 2009)

Obeng, Eddie, All Change! The Project Leader's Secret Handbook (Financial Times/ Prentice Hall: 1995)

Oshry, Barry, Seeing Systems: Unlocking the Mysteries of Organizational Life, (Berrett-Koehler, 1995).

Osterwalder, Alexander and Pigneur, Yves, Business Model Generation (Wiley: 2010)

Pink, Daniel, Drive: The Surprising Truth about What Motivates Us (Canongate Books: 2012)

- To Sell is Human: the surprising truth about persuading, convincing and influencing others (Canongate: 2013).

Reynolds, Garr, Presentation Zen: Simple Ideas on Presentation and Delivery (New Riders: 2011)

Rogers, Everett M., The Diffusion of Innovations (Simon & Schuster: 2004)

Schein, Edgar, Organizational Culture and Leadership (Jossey-Bass: 1985).

Schlesinger, Leonard A., Kiefer, Charles F., and Brown, Paul B., Just Start: Take Action, Embrace Uncertainty, Create the Future (Harvard Business Press: 2012)

Shannon, Claude E. & Warren Weaver (1949): A Mathematical Model of Communication. (University of Illinois Press: 1949)

Shaw, Patricia, Changing Conversations in Organizations: A Complexity Approach to Change (Complexity and Emergence in Organizations) (Routledge: 2002)

Sinek, Simon, Start with Why: How Great Leaders Inspire Everyone to take Action. (Portfolio Penguin: 2009).

Stokes, Patricia D., Creativity from Constraints: The Psychology of Breakthrough (Springer Publishing: 2005).

Wernham, Brian, Agile Project Management for Government: Leadership skills for implementation of large-scale public sector projects in months, not years (Maitland and Strong, 2012).

Zeldin, Theodore, Conversation: How Talk can Change our Lives (Hidden Spring, 2000).

Glossary

- **Ambivert**. Someone who can adjust between introversion and extroversion, allowing them to be more effective in influencing others.

- **Benefit**. Something seen as desirable or advantageous by one or more stakeholders.

- **Change Agenda**. All the change initiatives within an organisation, such as projects, programmes, marketing initiatives, and business unit changes. The change agenda is often rolled up and encapsulated into a portfolio management plan.

- **Communications Plan**. A plan of engagement events with stakeholders, their key media and messages, and how they coordinate with project milestones, as well as review milestones.

- **Customer Journey Map**. A description of all the experiences a customer has in transacting with an organisation and the emotions that are provoked because of this.

- **Deliverable**. See 'Output'.

- **Dis-benefit**. Something seen as disadvantageous or undesirable by one or more stakeholders.

- **Empathy**. The ability to read and understand another's feelings.

- **Empathy Map**. A visual analysis technique used for analysing a persona.

- **Engagement Strategy**. A considered approach by you and your team towards engaging the stakeholders in a coordinated way, with clearly understood protocols and measures.

- **Gatekeeper.** A stakeholder who holds power over your progress but is external to it. The power is usually to say "No."

- **Keystone habit**. A pivotal habit that informs shifts and reshapes other habits.

- **MBWA.** Managing by Wandering Around. A management practice that advocates a manager being physically present even when they do not have a formal pretext for being so, allowing them to observe practices and energy levels, as well as overhear conversations, all of which can help gain a better assessment of what is actually going on.

- **Model**. A generalised map of a management process or structure. It provides a workable simplification of a complex management environment.

- **Noise**. Anything heard in and around a communication that is not the intended content, which can distract from attention and comprehension by the receiver.

- **Off-Site Event**. Meeting away from usual working environments, to reduce the environmental noise, and allows people to focus.

- **Other-perspective**. The skill or ability to understand how someone thinks in a particular situation.

- **Outcome**. The result of a change, normally affecting behaviours and circumstances of people operating a transformed business.

- **Output**. Something tangible or verifiable that a project delivers to its customer.

- **Persona**. A fictional individual used to represent a group of people in order to understand them better.

- **Pitch**. Any summary form of the change proposition to a stakeholder, from one word, to a standard set of messages in a full-blown presentation.

- **Product**. The term for an Output used by PRINCE2 and other approaches.

- **Signal to Noise Ratio**. A measure of the clarity of a received signal, comparing extraneous noise with the signal over a communications medium.

- **Stakeholder**. Any individual or group that has an interest in or some influence over the project or its outcome.

- **Stakeholder Engagement**. The act of engaging with, and influencing stakeholders in and around a change or a project in the interests of improving the outcome and realising its benefits.

- **Stakeholder Engagement Strategy**. The document that assembles all aspects of the Stakeholder Engagement. See 'Stakeholder Engagement'.

- **Stakeholder Profile**. A co-ordinating record of one or more stakeholders that a team can use to share information and analysis on those stakeholders.

- **User Story**. One or more sentences in the everyday language of the end user or customer that captures what they do or needs to do as part of their job or function.

- **Vision**: A picture of a beneficial future, which is the result of one or more changes, usually in written form.

- **Wiki**. A document written and edited collaboratively, usually hosted on a web site.

- **WIIFM**. An acronym for "What's In It For Me?" a basic other-perspective reference.

Index

workshops 100
presentations 188–189, 220. *See also* pitches
pride 26. *See also* humility
'principle'
  defintion 24
principles of engagement 17, 22. *See also* seven principles of stakeholder
    engagement
products. *See* deliverables
profiling 120–122
  example profile 121
programmes
  MSP 25
  review 236
project assurance role 172
project management
  defining roles 171–172
  example of project organisation 171
  frame of reference 15–17
project managers
  high performing. *See also* high performing project managers
  role 172
project plan 192–193
projects. *See also* benefits
  as vehicle for change 28
  documentation, use of 192–193
  engagement of people pre-commencement 6
  execution of. *See* execution
  failure to deliver benefits 5–7, 12
  increase in 3
  lack of commitment, post-project 6
  review 235
  types 164–166
providers 101. *See also* stakeholders
purpose, need for 57–58

Q

question pitch 143. *See also* pitches

R

rapport 107
rationality/irrationality 39–40
Reicheld scale 236, 241
relational bank accounts 169

Lightning Source UK Ltd.
Milton Keynes UK
UKOW06f1623010915

257902UK00005B/16/P